OVERDUE

OVERDUE

Reckoning
with the
Public Library

AMANDA OLIVER

CHICAGO
REVIEW
PRESS

Copyright © 2022 by Amanda Oliver
All rights reserved
Published by Chicago Review Press Incorporated
814 North Franklin Street
Chicago, Illinois 60610
ISBN 978-1-64160-531-1

Library of Congress Control Number: 2021948373

Interior design: Nord Compo

Printed in the United States of America
5 4 3 2 1

For my parents
and all who have found themselves in a library

Of course they needed to care. It was the meaning of everything.

—Lois Lowry, *The Giver*

CONTENTS

AUTHOR'S NOTE

By now I am unfazed by the two familiar looks I see pass over people's faces when I share that I was a librarian for nearly seven years. There are, I swear to you, only two reactions. One is amusement and it is instant. A smile cracks and their mouth is already open, moving with words I can easily predict:

My librarian didn't look like you.

Does the Dewey Decimal System still exist?

Oh wow, so you get to read all day.

Where are your glasses? (If I am not wearing them.)

Now the glasses make sense! (If I am wearing them.)

The other reaction comes with a slower smile and, if I'm paying enough attention, a relaxing of their shoulders or a leaning in, like they instantly understand me better:

My friend/mom/cousin/uncle is a librarian and it's such a fascinating job.

I always thought I might want to be a librarian. Maybe when I retire.

That is so cool. What kind of library?

I now respond to both reactions with the same summary: My job as a librarian was wonderful and also incredibly challenging (perplexed faces from the first group and encouraging or curious nods from the second). Libraries are not the same as they were when we were younger (perplexed faces from the first group and encouraging or curious nods from the second). Libraries are so much more than books, and librarians are so much more than the people who mind the books (you get it by now).

If I am tired, I lie and say, "Yes, I did a lot of reading back then."

Librarians are not the outdated stereotypes that, somehow, still prevail on television, on podcasts, and in daily conversations: White women in cardigans and cat-eye glasses who wander spaces shushing patrons and placing books back on their shelves. Librarians are men, women, and nonbinary people. They are people of every race, though the field is still dominated by White librarians, especially in leadership roles. Most librarians are advocates. They are protectors and they are community resources. They are also citizens, community members, and individuals with their own personal experiences, morals, and biases that impact the communities they serve.

This book is everything I have to offer as evidence that many of our stories and understandings and beliefs around and about libraries and librarians are not only false but often damaging—to the individual and collective histories of library spaces and the people who operate them, and also to our collective history as humans and to the stories and roles we ascribe to ourselves and our institutions, especially in America.

I can't imagine these pages being read without including a note that most of them were written during the COVID-19 pandemic, from March of 2020 to June of 2021. I wrote from a small desk I periodically moved around a four hundred-square-foot apartment in the Mojave Desert of California twenty minutes outside Joshua Tree. My view rotated from windows that faced east toward Goat Mountain and windows that faced west toward acres of government-owned land mostly untouched by humans. The soundtrack to these pages consisted of scrub jays, mourning doves, verdins, and winds that blew in with such force that the air in the apartment got thick with dirt and desert if I forgot to close the windows.

I did not have in-person access to many of the libraries and librarians I reference in these pages and, much more excruciatingly, while I was writing I did not see my family and closest friends or the places and communities I love and have relied on for internal and external guidance.

So many of us were stripped down to the rawest and most essential pieces of ourselves during this time. I wrote from that place, and ultimately, I think it was for the better. Where, and how, this book came together is steeped in the collective and individual grief and the many internal and external alterations that the COVID-19 pandemic created globally. I wrote in a place, in a time, in a way that necessarily, but often painfully, altered my fundamental ways of thinking not just about libraries and my time as a librarian but about the world and how I exist in it.

Within this book there are stories of marginalized people without access whose stories have been unheard or ignored, but they are not "voiceless." No one is without a voice just because the majority have not been listening. I am not, nor would I ever try to be, a "voice for the voiceless." I have included some details of patrons' lives as I witnessed them and as they impacted my understanding of the relationship between libraries and their patrons. I write about them to the best of my abilities, research, and memories. It is not, and never will be, my place to tell patrons' stories. Their stories belong to them.

For ease, I often use the broad words "library" and "libraries" to refer to public libraries, as opposed to the more typical inclusions (school, academic, private, and special libraries) under these words. During my tenure at the DC Public Library, we were told to refer to patrons or library users as *customers*, but I do not use that term here, preferring *patron* or *library user* instead. I use the words *unhoused, houseless, houselessness,* and *experiencing houselessness* to describe people without secure and stable housing, unless I am directly quoting a person, title, or text. I do not believe anyone is *home*less, which is to say that so long as people are alive they have a home within themselves, and I recognize that this home may be a precious anchor. Unhoused people may also have a physical home somewhere that they are unable to safely or comfortably return to and/ or have strong memories of or ties to a home. I do not wish to lessen that connection.

I also want to make space here to acknowledge that the history I cover in these pages begins mostly in colonial America, during and after some of the country's earliest violent colonizing of its original land and peoples. The true earliest forms of public libraries and librarians in this country belong to the many tribes and tribe members who still inhabit the land and uphold the values of shared storytelling through oral and written traditions that are arguably much more powerful than our modern concepts of writing, communication, and knowledge organization.

The names and identifying details of all patrons, coworkers, past partners, and officers have been changed within these pages. It is never my intention to purposefully harm anyone with my words, but I have been a reader, a librarian, a writer—a human—long enough to understand that harm inevitably happens in writing, especially in nonfiction. No part of this book is intended to demonize, shame, or otherwise disparage specific persons, organizations, or institutions.

PART I

BECOMING

1

NORTHWEST ONE

Nothing is too ugly for this world, I think. It's just that
people pretend not to see.

—Terese Marie Mailhot, *Heart Berries*

THE DAY OF THE INCIDENT it had been only me and Ms. Williams at the
circulation desk. I was one month into the job and used to calling these
kinds of things "incidents" by then. The yelling was coming from the
Adult Fiction section, an area with four tables that made up the far-right
corner of the larger square that was the library. Walls of tall bookcases
made it into its own square, and it was impossible to see into it unless
you were standing right within it. Only one chair, tucked in between the
emergency exit and a single bookcase—the Fiction *A*'s—could be seen
from the circulation desk. A few weeks earlier, a patron had overdosed
while sitting in it, his skin already blue by the time someone at the desk
noticed and called 911.

I knew it was Christian who was yelling before I reached him. He
was a regular patron who kept his cell phone in a holster on his hip and
a Bluetooth piece in his ear, loudly taking frequent phone calls until an
employee would tell him to hang up or take it outside. The other two
people sitting at the table with him kept their eyes fixed down as he yelled
up at an older woman who was standing near him. I recognized her by
the long flowing dress and colorful silk headscarf she always wore, but
I did not know her name. The woman often annoyed other patrons by

asking to borrow items from them—a cell phone, a tissue, a bit of their food—and would hover until she got a yes. Whatever she had asked him for that day annoyed him to a point where he had been saying "fuck you" for a while, obviously angry, but I don't know that anyone expected what happened next.

Christian stood and used both of his hands to shove the woman backward as hard as he could. Her thin body flew into the wooden bench behind her and her head audibly cracked on contact before she rolled to the floor.

I instantly started to yell. "Out! Out! Get out!"

The other patrons finally looked up, most of them staring at me. I was the woman with pink hair, the newest hire who was usually the most patient and friendly at the circulation desk, yet here I was now, angry and yelling.

Christian turned toward me, shouting how he'd done nothing and I didn't know shit. Spit was flying from his mouth. Two patrons I didn't know were cradling the woman's head as she lay sprawled out on the floor next to the bench. I tried to check for blood while simultaneously watching Christian.

"Bitch, you don't fucking know me," he said, this time pointing two fingers in my face. "I'll be waiting for you after your shift. I'll be right outside." He kept jabbing the air with his fingers, closer and closer to my face.

How many times had I been called a bitch that week? Five times? Ten? I knew meeting aggression with aggression rarely ended well, but here I was. Christian yelled and I yelled back and we moved toward the exit. The incident reminded me of one from many years ago when I was in high school. I had dated someone who tried to attack me outside a party a few weeks after we broke up as I was waiting in the back seat of a two-door Pontiac Sunfire while friends went inside to check if the coast was clear for me to come in. We had all been invited, but Stew did not want me anywhere near him if I wasn't "his." I had not expected what happened next then, either, which was that he came flying out of the front door of the house toward the car. I scrambled to reach for the window crank of the driver's door from the back seat, but his fists came in at me anyway. Two of his fellow football players were close behind and pulled him off. I knew that Stew was capable of violence, but I hadn't expected he would turn it on me. I felt the same way about Christian and a few other regulars at Northwest One. There was always this state of waiting to see.

Three of my coworkers had appeared from the back room and shadowed Christian and me silently, prepared to intervene if necessary. They could see I had snapped. Each one of them had, too, but this was my first time. Christian was long gone before we had a chance to discuss calling Library Police, and he was miles away by the time they finally arrived. But he kept his word to me for the next two days: at the end of my shifts he was just across the street, standing, waiting, watching. On the third day, he followed me and two coworkers on a mile-long walk to a restaurant, keeping pace on the opposite side of the street. When I finally looked over, he was staring back at me.

———

Libraries are often referred to in warm language: safe place, sanctuary, freedom granting, for all. There is the famous Jorge Luis Borges quote: "I have always imagined that Paradise will be a kind of library." And similar sentiments from Albert Einstein: "The only thing that you absolutely have to know, is the location of the library." From Ray Bradbury: "Without libraries what have we? We have no past and no future."[1] From Judy Blume: "I think of libraries as safe havens for intellectual freedom. I think of how many times I've been told about a librarian who saved a life by offering the right book at the right time."[2] And Margaret Atwood: "There is not such a cradle of democracy upon the earth as the Free Public Library."[3]

Warm understandings of libraries have long permeated our media as well: the *Breakfast Club* members find comradery in their school library, Hermione and Harry and Ron discover life-saving solutions and spells at the Hogwarts Library, Belle finds sanctuary and a sense of Beast's humanity in his private library, librarian Mrs. Phelps offers Matilda the beginning of her exit from an abusive home, the cast of *The Magicians* frequent the library for answers and deep conversations, and so on.

There is nothing incorrect about any of these beautiful assertions or imagined scenarios. But there remains a somewhat perplexing overarching social assumption that libraries are social equalizers and asylums from the rest of the world in ways that no other American institutions quite are—that libraries are *good*, as opposed to the *bad* we sometimes ascribe to museums and other shared spaces that have been criticized for being elitist and otherwise exclusionary or fraught.

When I tell someone for the first time that I was a librarian for six years, their face often lights up. Sometimes they want to tell me about their childhood library, or the last time they went to their local branch, or ask if I've read a particular book. Sometimes they just want to know what the work was *really* like. Was it quiet all the time? Did I read books all day? Did I have to go to school for that? Do I have glasses? Did I *shhh*?

They often tell me, last, about how much they love libraries. I tell them I do too.

And I do.

But I have stood in these conversations knowing that there are glaring omissions from their questions about, and their understandings of, libraries. This leaves me with the same general dilemma again and again: do I tell them something a little truer?

In my own social circles, I don't know anyone who doesn't like libraries, even if they haven't patronized one in decades. According to the American Library Association's (ALA) *State of America's Libraries Report 2019*, there are more public libraries—16,568—in the United States than Starbucks cafés—14,606. One hundred percent of those public libraries provide Wi-Fi and nearly 100 percent offer no-fee access to computers.[4] The ALA's 2020 report notes that "the popularity of libraries is surging" and cites a 2019 Gallup survey poll that visiting the library is the most common cultural activity Americans engage in "by far," with US adults taking an average of 10.5 trips a year to the library, "a frequency that exceeded their participation in eight other common leisure activities. Americans attended live music or theatrical events and visited national or historic parks roughly four times a year on average and visited museums and gambling casinos 2.5 times annually."[5]

The State of America's Libraries reports are released during National Library Week every April as annual summaries of library trends, and they include statistics and issues affecting all types of libraries, including public ones. The *State of America's Libraries Report 2019* notably states that public libraries "are a microcosm of the larger society. They play an important and unique role in the communities that they serve and provide an inclusive environment where all are treated with respect and dignity. No longer just places for books, our public libraries serve as a lifeline for some of our nation's most vulnerable communities." The report goes on to note that "homelessness and addiction are two of the most difficult issues facing communities today. They often go hand in hand."[6]

The ALA notes on its website that "[unhoused people] face a wide range of challenges including lack of affordable housing, employment opportunities, healthcare, and other needed services. As many public librarians know, with no safety net to speak of, homeless citizens often turn to the library for help."[7] It is common for libraries to be patronized by marginalized and vulnerable groups, whether they are in rural, suburban, or city settings, for a wide variety of reasons including free access to a temperature-controlled environment, clean drinking water, and Wi-Fi, and computers—because, of course, all public libraries are shared spaces. They do not exclude anyone, including people suffering from addiction, trauma, mental health struggles, and other internal, and often externalized, battles.

That unhoused people regularly patronize libraries has become more commonly known in recent years and is a fact that impacts some library users' desire to visit certain branches in their local library systems. Although there is no statistic on this, my own experience working within the DC Public Library system showed me time and again that the majority of middle- and upper-class library patrons who wanted to sit and work at a library preferred to visit branches in certain neighborhoods around the District over others, even if it was not their closest neighborhood branch. These same people *would* comfortably pick up holds from their local branch because it did not require them to linger in the space, but they opted for other libraries if they wanted to stay for longer than a few minutes. I have close friends in New York City, Portland, Seattle, Bethlehem, Buffalo, and DC who have similar practices and preferences. Some of them take their children to library story times as well, but again, there are branches in their local library systems where they would choose not to take their children and where they would prefer not to pick up books or try to work, whether that is something they can comfortably admit or not.

It is obvious through data that libraries are still regularly used all over the country by people from all races and socioeconomic statuses, but the reasons they use libraries differ greatly. While library usage remains statistically prevalent and on the rise, I continue to be interested in the question of by whom, where, and for what reasons.

Two weeks before Christian assaulted the woman, I had been in the Adult Fiction area reshelving books. The collection was disorganized—a side effect not so much of being understaffed, but of staff never agreeing whose job it was to reshelve—and the disarray often doubled how long it took to find the correct place for books on the shelf. Generally, I didn't mind reshelving, but I tried to never linger in the area. Male coworkers had warned me early on not to—female employees were particularly vulnerable back there. If something was going to go wrong, it was going to go wrong in the Adult Fiction area.

I was on my tiptoes that day, impatiently searching spines for the letters *PAT* when I heard him from behind me.

"There's my White girl with a booty."

I went momentarily stiff and then shrank the only way I could shrink in the moment—back down to flat feet, arms crossed protectively over my chest, book pinned against my sternum with my pointer finger hooked slightly on the plastic of the spine label, pressing my flesh into it. I had spent most of my adult life trying to avoid this exact situation: feeling cornered and vulnerable, especially around men. There was laughter—three, four, five male echoes of it—and I moved my body sideways instead of turning around to look. I tossed the James Patterson paperback on an otherwise emptied cart and beelined to our small back office.

This was different from the times I had been harassed at the circulation desk. The circ desk was familiar territory and its height gave me a sense of having some physical boundary. Christian had made flirtatious comments there before, leaning against the desk to tell me how nice my hair was and then, a few days later, asking me if I had a boyfriend, but nothing this inappropriate, demeaning, and public. Our previous interactions were harmless enough—the kind of conversations I'd had with hundreds of men while sitting on a barstool before a friend arrived for happy hour or standing waiting for a delayed Metro train. I could deflect—answer in short replies, busy myself with organizing something on the desk's surface, respond that I needed to get back to my work, show them the subway face I had developed while living in New York City—but this was my workplace, and Christian was someone I knew I would be seeing on a regular basis. Northwest One was a weekly, if not daily, part of his life.

When I got into the back office my manager, Frank, was sitting in front of his two computers. "I just want to tell you about something that just happened," I began, speaking to his back. It was the first time I had ever come to him like this. He knew by my voice that I was angry, and when he turned, he saw my face was red. Frank arranged himself into what I had started to think of as his "listening pose": direct eye contact, square shoulders, softened face. Neutral. Listening.

"Christian made a comment while I was trying to reshelve books. This isn't the first time he's made me uncomfortable, and I'm not really sure what to do at this point."

I was hoping Frank would know what to do. He had been working in public libraries for almost ten years, and I had very little experience at that point, having recently transitioned from six years in elementary school libraries.

"What did he say?"

I repeated the line, and Frank frowned and nodded sympathetically. "You know, in his culture, that's a compliment."

I stood there silently. Christian was a Latino man. Frank was White. I didn't know how to respond to the comment or the fact that Frank seemed to think I simply wasn't understanding the situation correctly. Until that moment, he had always made me feel like he empathized with the many layers of being a female employee at Northwest One. His wife worked at another library and sometimes called during her shifts, clearly upset. Caller ID on the government phones showed the name of her branch, and if I saw the call come in, I tried to answer before it rang more than a few times, thinking how each ring must have made her feel more helpless and alone. I'd heard Frank be gentle and understanding with her on these calls, and so I stood silent, hopeful, still, waiting for what he might say next.

"I can try to go talk to him if you'd like, but . . ." he trailed off.

I blinked and stood for a few more moments before I told Frank something along the lines of "OK, never mind," and went back out onto the library floor. Years of similar situations—at school, at work, in private and public—passed through my mind, but I compartmentalized them and sat down at a chair behind the circulation desk. Christian stayed where he was.

With years of distance, I now more fully understand there is another story here of Christian's life. In some ways, Frank had been correct. There was a difference in our lived experiences. Christian had learned to respond to both affronts and minor annoyances with violence, and there is no calm or peaceful way to learn that. He acted, spoke, and behaved in ways that made sense to him. I did the same, trying to maintain the relative sense of safety I had established in my adult life, feeling like I deserved at least that. If we had anything in common, it was this—a desire to protect ourselves.

These incidents with Christian were two of hundreds of incidents with dozens of patrons in the nine months that I worked at Northwest One. In all of them, there was self-protection at play for everyone involved. It was a shared experience I could find no comfort in. Our common ground came from operating in a shared environment that was unsafe. There was never any reliable way to predict what might happen next at Northwest One, no matter how hard I, or anyone else, tried to. And when things inevitably came to a head, there was no reliable plan of response in place either. This has become a common story of libraries and library work in America.

I have upset people, from library administrators and other librarians to journalists and close friends, by candidly discussing my job as a librarian at the Northwest One branch of the Washington, DC, public library system. When I explain the reality of the work and the many ways it embodies the most fractured pieces of American society and culture, I push directly against the romanticization of what libraries are and who they are for. It is complicated to hear and it is also complicated to share. But as with most broadly accepted accounts of American history and culture, there are extensive misunderstandings and omissions from the story that have become especially difficult to sit with.

We want, and need, institutions that embody hope—now more than ever. Public libraries, maybe above all else, have a long history of providing just that. And there *is* deep and resounding hope in libraries and library work. But if that hope expects to grow and evolve, it is essential that a full and accurate story be told.

Famed astronomer and astrophysicist Carl Sagan hits a little closer to a more complete truth about libraries: "The health of our civilization, the depth of our awareness about the underpinnings of our culture and our concern for the future can all be tested by how well we support our libraries."[8]

Libraries are resolutely radical institutions. They are free to use and open to the public, spaces that demand nothing from you to enter and nothing for you to stay. No exchange of money occurs between library user and library, save for overdue book fees, which are becoming more and more obsolete. Libraries are sanctuaries for the mind, body, and spirit. They are repositories of language, literature, community care, and human growth. And they are also places of objectification, racism, sexual assault, and other human atrocities. They are embodiments of our history and culture, for better, and also for worse.

It can be uncomfortable to think of libraries as social institutions that plainly tell the many layered stories of racism, classism, and deep-rooted neglect of marginalized and vulnerable populations in our communities and across our nation. It is perhaps even more uncomfortable to think of libraries as places that house specific and horrifying incidents of trauma and violence. But to continue to laud libraries and librarians as ever-present equalizers and providers of some version of magic reduces them to something wistfully—and sometimes dangerously—negligible. It also inevitably prevents them from making meaningful changes and progress. We can continue to broadly (and *rightly*) accept that libraries are open to everyone in society and deserve praise for what they embody. But to keep doing so from a removed view—and often from the brief and incomplete perspectives of the most advantaged people—is a disservice to the true scope of the work libraries and librarians are doing.

Without an understanding of a more complete history of the American public library it is impossible to accurately and productively discuss their current state. It is impossible to move forward without meaningfully and purposefully looking back. This kind of reflection, the kind born from inquiry and research and telling, from deep, honest reckoning, cannot be fully realized without examining it more closely. I think of Sagan's words often: "the depth of our awareness about the underpinnings of our culture." A shallow depth, one with an insufficient or incomplete awareness and understanding, has led to the problematic idea of libraries as institutions that allow all people to pull themselves up by their metaphorical bootstraps.

I can't think of a better metaphor for our country—where it has been, where it is now, and where it is headed or could be headed—than in the story of our libraries. Libraries hold possibilities and answers for our future in ways no other institutions do. I believe this as a former librarian trained in the gathering, assessment, and accessibility of information, and also as a writer who seeks to put it all together in a cohesive narrative. I believe this as a human being, to my core. In the space I have created since leaving library work for good, in the parts of me that are most calm, observant, and present.

2

OMNIUM LUX CIVIUM

What happens when you let an unsatisfactory present go
on long enough? It becomes your entire history.

—Louise Erdrich

THE HISTORY OF THE AMERICAN PUBLIC LIBRARY has been told before,
in many places, and it is not difficult to understand that it is intimately
tied to virtually all critical moments in American history including mass
genocides of Indigenous Americans, American colonialism and imperial-
ism, immigration and the impacts of efforts to create "Americanization,"
segregation and the civil rights movements of the 1950s and 1960s, gender
gaps, gatekeeping in higher education, and our country's unending and
violent history of racism. These connections are essential to name and
recognize. But it is the discarded and lesser-told histories and stories of
people, many of whom have collided in some way with society, that I
find more important to understanding how time has passed and how
the world has changed.

It is often a librarian's job to make sense of information exactly like
this: in pieces, from parts, across decades or centuries, sorted and organized
into a collective whole that is, ideally, inclusive and accessible. Or at least
to gather reliable resources to help patrons make their own connections.

The more I learned about the public library, the more clearly I saw
my own errors and transgressions within it. The more I encountered
deep and uncomfortable *guilt*.

And herein lies a truth about American history: we have traditionally not just avoided its more uncomfortable and difficult pieces but omitted and even denied them altogether. I have no desire to continue that practice here.

What follows is a collection of information I found in my research that I see as essential to creating a baseline understanding of how American libraries began and how they have existed until this point in time. My hope is that it might help us move into new connections and understandings of not just what libraries have taught, but what they can continue to teach us through a more robust and inclusive understanding of them.

—————————

The earliest free public library in America is generally accepted to be the Library Company of Philadelphia, founded by Benjamin Franklin in 1731. In childhood, Franklin read extensively and used what money he had to purchase books, going so far as a teenager to stop eating meat to have more money for them. In adulthood, Franklin formed the Junto Club with a group of White, middle-class Philadelphia men. Junto members met on Friday evenings for weekly meetings that started with one of twenty-four questions they were encouraged to ask themselves on the morning of each gathering. (A few of those questions: What new story have you lately heard agreeable for telling in conversation? Have you late heard of any citizen's thriving well, and by what means? Is there any difficulty in matters of opinion, of justice, and injustice, which you would gladly have discussed at this time?[1])

These twelve tradesmen and artisans—carpenters, scholars, scribes, metalworkers—gathered first in a local tavern and later in their private homes with the shared hope that honing their collective skills would improve their lives and positions within the community, as well as the society they lived in overall. They were interested in discussing issues of morals, policies, and natural philosophy in what they called their "society of mutual improvement,"[2] with one of their first undertakings being the development and regulation of a city watch they proposed be funded by taxes collected from landowners in proportion to the size of their property. Junto members regularly needed to look up information in books during their weekly discussions, and in the early days, members pooled their own books to create a shared collection. Eventually, members wanted their books back in their homes for personal use, though. When this was expressed, I imagine the group gathered and asked one of those twenty-four questions: how might this be amended?

It was Franklin who proposed a subscription library as the solution and his friend conveyancer Charles Brockden who drew up the papers outlining its policies. Each member paid a sum for the first purchase of books and then paid an annual contribution of forty shillings—a week's salary for many of the members—moving forward. Fifty of them agreed to pay it, and the Library Company of Philadelphia was officially born, with books bought and imported from Europe and the library open once a week to its members. If books were not returned on time, the borrower owed the library twice its original cost, thus creating the first overdue fee system. Franklin eventually realized that having to contribute forty shillings for access to the library was a burden for some, and the company made a new bylaw that men who weren't shareholders could still borrow the books if they left a deposit of twice the value of the book with the librarian. White women who had husbands or brothers who were shareholders could borrow as well. In his autobiography, Franklin wrote that the libraries that began to grow after his initial inception of the Library Company "improved the general Conversation of Americans, made the common Tradesmen and Farmers as intelligent as most Gentlemen from other Countries, and perhaps have contributed in some Degree to the Stand so generally made throughout the Colonies in Defence of their Privileges."[3]

All people of color were barred from accessing the Library Company, and, for all of Benjamin Franklin and the Junto Club's members' interest in discourse and community betterment, for all the almost nauseatingly extensive and carefully kept and preserved records of their work, there is no documented, or even implied debate or interest, in discussing access for people who were not White or from a certain social class. This, of course, reflects the general attitudes and behaviors of colonial America. When Franklin and his peers founded the Library Company, teaching an enslaved person how to read was still illegal and punishable by death. Indigenous Americans were also forbidden access, though many had already been forcibly displaced and relocated from Pennsylvania to midwestern territories by then. White indentured servitude was also common in colonial Philadelphia, and people in these groups—mostly women who were cultural and racial minorities, as well as the poor—were regarded as inferior to affluent White men and barred from accessing materials from most early libraries. Literacy was also a limiting factor, as education was reserved for middle- and upper-class White people. Even as access to education became more accessible to lower classes, and more of a public matter of concern, many students had to resign from school early to help work to support their parents and siblings in the aftermath of the Civil War. There is also minimal recorded information about the Philadelphia Library Company of Colored Persons, but its founding in 1833 makes it clear that all citizens understood the value of access to libraries and wanted to benefit from them too.

The story of the earliest library in America—one dominated by Whiteness, privilege, and exclusion, however conventional it was then— paved the way for much of how public libraries would look for the next two hundred years.

Thumbtacked to the wall above my desk is a printed etching from the early 1800s of a smiling man heating a pan over a candle flame. He is wearing a yellow tailcoat and breeches and an apron, with his legs bent like a frog's. It's silly, especially for its time, and that's part of why I printed it. It serves as a visual reminder that the founding of public libraries involved many more people than Benjamin Franklin and Andrew Carnegie.

The man in the photo—dressed up as one of his many characters, "Nicholas"—was a successful French ventriloquist named Nicholas Marie Alexandre Vattemare who traveled throughout the world with his act in the early-to-mid-1800s. He also played a significant role in the development and founding of early American libraries. In 1839, Vattemere traveled from France to America with his act and arranged a meeting with the privately funded Mercantile Library Association of Boston. He had seen the importance and communal good of sharing books in countries all over the world and suggested a shared library between France and the United States. Those in attendance unanimously passed a resolution supporting the project. At the same time Vattemare was working on his vision, Harvard professors George Ticknor and Edward Everett were working on their own ideas for a library, hoping to provide reading materials to all Boston citizens. Ticknor, in particular, championed the circulation of popular fiction, a genre that eventually helped draw to public libraries millions of users who had otherwise been disinterested by most early library collections. Between the professors, Vattemare, and the Boston mayor's support, City Document no. 37 came to life, outlining how and why there should be a tax-funded library with an elected president, rules, regulations, and fundraising ideas.[4] It was the first document of its kind, and educators and investors from all over the world sent money or wrote in their support. Joshua Bates, a London banker, read a copy of it and sent $50,000 for the new library, writing to ask that it only be spent if the library "shall be an ornament to the city" and include reading rooms. He elaborated that "it will not do to have the rooms in the proposed library much inferior to the rooms occupied for the same object by the upper classes. Let the virtuous and industrious of the middle and mechanic class feel that such a place is free to him."[5]

The first American public library opened at a schoolhouse on Mason Street in Boston at 9:00 in the morning on March 20, 1854. The library stayed open until 9:30 that night, serving eighty visitors throughout the day. By the end of the year, there were 6,590 registered library users who frequented the library. In 1870 a second branch opened, and the Boston Public Library (BPL) became the first American branch library system.

It was at this point that the BPL adopted its motto: *Omnium lux civium*, Latin for "The Light of All People."

Dark and light dualism has a history of metaphorical use that goes as far back as the ancient Near East. The Genesis creation narrative has God separating "light from darkness" on his first day. The Dark Ages were marked by economic, intellectual, and cultural decline while the Age of Enlightenment centered around the pursuit of happiness, reason, liberty, and progress. Death is black in Homer's *Iliad*. White signifies virtue, virginity, and innocence in the Book of Revelation. Light and dark continue to function as deep metaphors, and binary oppositions, for an unending list of sociocultural dividing lines in our contemporary society. And the *light* mostly wealthy White men envisioned and etched into the foundation of public libraries did not reach everyone, nor was it intended to.

As public and private libraries continued to grow in popularity and spread across America throughout the 1800s, White men from New England's elite families were the predominant players. Women from the elite classes volunteered at libraries as well, particularly with children, but it was not until after 1900 that women began to dominate the day-to-day work of libraries. The public library's gendered history underpins the founding of the American Library Association (ALA), the first and largest library professional organization in the world. In the fall of 1876, 103 librarians from across the country—ninety men and thirteen women—met and determined that the mission of the ALA would be "to enable librarians to do their present work more easily and at less expense." In 1904, librarian Mary Cutler Fairchild openly noted that participation by women in ALA meetings was disproportionate to their attendance and that women greatly outnumbered men in the field. Women held a large amount of administrative positions, but with little administrative responsibility, and for lower salaries than their male colleagues. Library schools were, however, among the first professional curricula to regularly accept female applicants, and an estimated 75 percent of public libraries were brought into existence through Women's Clubs activism.[6] Not surprisingly, though, these clubs were run by wealthy, well-connected White women who barred women who were Jewish, Black, or part of the working poor. Again, these marginalized groups responded, believing access to libraries was a basic human right. In 1896, the National Association of Colored Women's Clubs (NACWC) was formed and began to champion public libraries, bringing books to communities and children who couldn't access major city libraries. It was not until the late 1930s that the ALA started to adopt policies designed to combat discrimination, including sexism, within libraries. The Library Bill of Rights was established on June 19, 1939, stating that "a person's right to use a library should not be denied or abridged because of origin, age, background, or views."[7]

As advocacy for library access increased and the Progressive Era ushered in a spirit of improving society, including public education, calls for building public libraries grew even more. The funding for many of these early libraries came from Andrew Carnegie, who had first come to the United States from Scotland in 1848 when he was twelve years old. Carnegie immediately started working as a bobbin boy in an Allegheny City textile mill at a low-paying wage for his manual labor. Wanting to make more money than he did, Carnegie believed the books available at the local Colonel James Anderson's library could be his pathway out of poverty, but only apprentices and tradesmen were permitted access to the library. Carnegie pled his case in a letter to the library's administrators: he was a young man, a working man, but not yet an apprentice, and he believed he could improve his career trajectory if he had access to the library's collection of how-to books. He received a quick reply denying him special access, but, undeterred, Carnegie got the letter published in the *Pittsburgh Dispatch*, signing it "Working Boy." The library administrators were impressed by his continued efforts and not only gave Carnegie access but also opened the library to working men in Philadelphia. In his autobiography, Carnegie wrote how he "resolved, if wealth ever came to me, that it should be used to establish free libraries."[8] Between 1883 and 1929, he gave over $60 million of his wealth to fund a system of nearly 1,700 public libraries across the United States.

This is part of the common story of the founding of America's public libraries. This is the history I find not just dry and somewhat boring to unpack, but also slightly maddening. When I dug for the "who else?" in early library history the results were mostly what I have already outlined here: demographics, not individuals. I continued to look for the common people, the innovators, and the outliers, but they were much harder to find. Each time I encountered Franklin or Ticknor or Carnegie, I landed back on the *light*. Who was it for?

Carnegie-funded libraries were engraved with an image of a rising sun and similar words as those above the Boston Public Library: LET THERE BE LIGHT. This *light*, again, did not reach everyone, nor was it intended to. Financial backers and librarians who played integral roles in the early founding of public libraries often viewed libraries and librarians like missionaries, believing that their existence—both of libraries and of

White people—could bring "civilization" and reform through libraries and library work. The light they gave expected that the recipients looked, behaved, and believed in specific ways. It was not meant to shine on everyone, despite what the granite and marble said.

This exclusivity extended to the more than twenty million immigrants who came to the United States between 1880 and 1920. The ALA's Committee on Work with the Foreign Born published a series of well-meaning guidebooks for adapting collections to meet the needs of immigrants, starting with *The Polish Immigrant and His Reading* in 1924. Eventually there were also German, Greek, and Italian volumes. The guides listed suggested titles for librarians to purchase to attract immigrants to libraries and gave tips about serving people from other cultural backgrounds. Many libraries purchased foreign-language collections they believed reflected the interests and needs of the populations arriving from Europe and, in some states, from Japan, Mexico, Puerto Rico, and the Philippines. Public librarians in some parts of the country also made holistic changes to library programming to engage immigrants. In 1921, Pura Belpré, New York City's first Puerto Rican librarian, transformed the New York Public Library's 115th Street branch into a vibrant community center for newly arrived Puerto Rican immigrants by purchasing Spanish-language books, leading bilingual story hours, and offering programs on traditional holidays.

Between 1900 and 1915, more than fifteen million immigrants arrived in the United States, and unlike earlier immigrants, the majority were from non-English-speaking European countries. In a series of cases that began in 1901, the Supreme Court assigned the status of "nationals" rather than "citizens" to immigrants from southern and eastern Europe, especially Italy, Poland, and Russia. Their cultures and languages were often more foreign to Americans than those of immigrants from western Europe, and groups from these countries were not considered White at the time, while immigrants from western European countries like England, the Netherlands, Ireland, Germany, and Scandinavian countries were. Collective calls for something to "be done" about the perceived problems of these differences were heeded by libraries and librarians all over the country who distributed Americanization Registration Cards that required a signature agreeing to "the use of a common language," "the elimination of disorder and unrest," and "the maintenance of an American standard of living through the proper use of American foods, care of children and new world homes."[9] This focus on "Americanization" aimed to make immigrants conform to American norms and customs with an implication that their own norms and customs were inferior. Through this work, libraries and librarians aided in the eradication of the culture, language, and customs immigrants brought with them to their new home, erasing lifetimes of history. Knowing that Black citizens fared even worse than them, the majority of these immigrants chose to embrace Whiteness and demonstrate their cultural and biological "fitness" to be White citizens, further upholding and protecting the already deeply established White supremacy, segregation, and diminutions of Black citizens.[10]

Perhaps the least honestly examined discrimination and exclusion that public libraries and librarians have enforced is the violent and devastating segregation of Black populations. Throughout the 1800s, individual states and federal and local segregation laws largely denied people who were Black access to public libraries. In the 1896 case *Plessy v. Ferguson,* the Supreme Court upheld "separate but equal" facilities as constitutional, legally justifying the creation of segregated public spaces for Black Americans. Between 1908 and 1924, twelve segregated "Colored Carnegie Libraries" opened in smaller buildings, with fewer books and significantly less funding than Carnegie libraries for White people.

Rev. Thomas Fountain Blue was selected to lead one of these libraries in 1905 in Louisville, Kentucky. Born in Farmville, Virginia, to formerly enslaved parents, Reverend Blue oversaw the first library in the country to be run by an entirely African American staff. In 1914, Blue opened Louisville's second Carnegie branch library intended for African Americans to use. More than just a site for circulating books, both of Blue's branches served as community centers with sponsored educational programs. Despite Blue's being a pioneer in the movement to make libraries community anchors, his revolutionary history is often excluded from the story of libraries in America. This is also the case when it comes to the integral contributions of other Black librarians, including Clara Stanton Jones, Virginia Lacy Jones, E. J. Josey, and Albert P. Marshall—all of whom led desegregation efforts and created immense progress in library work overall.

Across the United States, the trend of tax-funded public libraries continued to grow, with segregated reading rooms for Black populations within White-only libraries beginning to more regularly replace separate libraries. Some southern cities and towns provided marginal service to Black communities through things like traveling bookmobiles and admittance of Black populations to their local library once a week while it was closed to White patrons, but access to libraries remained deeply segregated throughout the early 1900s. Many Black citizens fought tirelessly against this.

On August 21, 1939, activists attempted to desegregate the public library in Alexandria, Virginia, less than ten miles from DC. The public library on Queen Street was situated in the heart of one of the city's Black neighborhoods, and five Black men arrived at its doors that morning to request a library card. All of them were refused. Instead of exiting, they walked into the stacks, selected books, and sat down at separate tables to read. The library page on duty ran to the home of head librarian Catharine Scoggin and yelled, "Oh mercy, Miss Scoggin, there's colored people all over the library."[11] As three hundred spectators gathered outside the library, Scoggin consulted with the city manager and police officers. The men were placed under arrest for disorderly conduct. Samuel W. Tucker, a twenty-six-year-old attorney, had organized the sit-in after learning about the power of nonviolent protests from a teacher who studied with Mahatma Gandhi. Historians have since noted that if he hadn't staged the demonstration it would have taken far longer before Black Alexandrians could use a library. Despite his efforts, the Alexandria Library did not become fully desegregated until over twenty years later, in 1962.

Again, again, I return to the light. That false invocation and promise of light.

By 1946, just under one-third of the public library systems in the South reported some form of service to Black Americans. Despite a lack of funds, materials, and often autonomy, these libraries provided otherwise unavailable or expensive reading content to their patrons and formed important community spaces. During the civil rights movement of the 1950s and 1960s, segregated public libraries were regularly challenged through nonviolent and carefully coordinated protests. On March 27, 1961, nine members of the local NAACP Youth Council attempted to use the White-only Jackson, Mississippi, public library. When they refused to leave, they were arrested and jailed for disturbing the peace. Over the next two years, similar protests occurred at local libraries across the South, with some ending more violently than others. On September 15, 1963, two African American ministers, Rev. William B. McClain and Rev. Nimrod Quintus Reynolds, were attacked and severely beaten by a White mob as they attempted to integrate Alabama's Anniston Public Library on the corner of downtown 10th Street and Wilmer Avenue, a library that was built with the help of matching funds from Andrew Carnegie.[12] A library with the words LET THERE BE LIGHT etched into it loomed above them as they were attacked.

In 1964 the Civil Rights Act specifically outlawed discrimination in public accommodations, including public libraries, and the Voting Rights Act of 1965 then gave African Americans full access to vote, granting them power in local government, public facilities, and, finally, public libraries. The implementation of these laws was still mercilessly slow.

In 1964 Teri Moncure Mojgani, most recently a librarian at Xavier University of Louisiana, participated in a protest at the public library in Hattiesburg, Mississippi. She described the experience in 2018 on a panel titled "Hidden Figures in American Library History" at the main branch of the New Orleans Public Library: how a young woman at the circulation desk looked up, saw Mojgani and a small group of peaceful protesters, and immediately left the circulation desk to call for help. When an older librarian asked the group what they wanted, they replied that they wanted library cards. They were told that the library was only for White people, to which one of the members of the group replied, "But our parents pay taxes, and there's this law now. You have to let us use the library."

Maintaining their original stance, the librarians said that if the peaceful protestors stayed, they would call police. As we see from testimonies like Mojgani's, the public libraries in the South that did provide limited and inferior services to Black people in the 1950s and '60s often subjected them to experiences that were humiliating.[13]

Mojgani was joined on the 2018 panel in New Orleans by three other Black activists who had protested segregated libraries in the South. All had been invited by organizers Wayne and Shirley Wiegand, husband and wife librarians, professors, and authors of *The Desegregation of Public Libraries in the Jim Crow South*. The event came shortly after the ALA passed a 2018 resolution titled Resolution to Honor African Americans Who Fought Library Segregation, or CD#41. The resolution was created to apologize "to African Americans for wrongs committed against them in segregated public libraries."[14]

The wording of the apology leans toward legalese throughout:

> Whereas, in many cases the American Library Association participated, both passively and actively, in the disenfranchisement of African American librarians, depriving them of the resources of professional association;
>
> Whereas the American Library Association continued to accept segregated public libraries as members into the 1960s;
>
> Whereas the American Library Association filed no amicus curiae briefs in any of the local, state, and national lawsuits filed in the 1950s and 1960s to desegregate public libraries;
>
> Whereas the nation's library press reported nothing about the 1939 Alexandria (VA) Library sit-in by five young African Americans that took place two months after the American Library Association passed a Library Bill of Rights;
>
> Whereas a sincere and heartfelt apology is an important and necessary first step in the process of reconciliation;
>
> Whereas an apology for decades of injustices cannot erase the past, but a recognition of the wrongs committed and injustices ignored can help the nation's library community confront the ghosts of its past: Now, therefore, be it
>
> Resolved, That the American Library Association

(1) Acknowledges the fundamental injustice, cruelty, and inhumanity of racially segregated libraries;

(2) Apologizes to African Americans for wrongs committed against them in segregated public libraries;

(3) Commends African Americans who risked their lives to integrate public libraries for their bravery and courage in challenging segregation in public libraries and in forcing public libraries to live up to the rhetoric of their ideals;

(4) Welcomes all African Americans to libraries, recognizing in particular those who were forced to use segregated libraries;

(5) Encourages libraries to defend, in their policies and in their actions, the *ALA Code of Ethics* principle 1—"We provide the highest level of service to all library users through appropriate and usefully organized resources; equitable access; and accurate, unbiased, and courteous responses to all requests";

(6) Will review policy documents and internal procedures to ensure Equity, Diversity, and Inclusion (EDI) principles are reflected throughout, and;

(7) And be it further resolved that this resolution be printed in full in *American Libraries* and publicized widely via all media channels.

When I first read CD#41, I could not help thinking of poet Layli Long Soldier's 2017 debut poetry collection *Whereas*. Long Soldier's book was a direct response to the Congressional Resolution of Apology to Native Americans (S. J. Res. 14, 111th Congress [2009–2010]) that President Barack Obama signed in 2009.

The apology was a minor inclusion in section 8113 of the 2010 Department of Defense Appropriations Act.[15] The apology was embedded in legislative preparations for war. No Native Americans were present to receive the apology when it was signed. The entire document is 1,290 words and the word *whereas* makes up twenty of them.

In the discourse of a contract or a treaty, a *whereas* clause is an introductory statement that means something akin to "because" or "considering that." In the discourse of law, *whereas* signals important context in a formal or contractual document—but it also represents nonbinding language.[16] Long Soldier confronts the coercive language in the collection and shows how words themselves, especially government legalese, can be used as tools of oppression.

That an apology for years of systematic segregation and racism in libraries only came to be written in 2018 is astonishing, especially given that libraries are institutions that house thousands of years of history and librarians are experts in the dissemination of information, not to mention that the ALA is the largest and longest-running library association in not just the United States but the world. The legal jargon of the apology adds, at very best, a level of authority or seriousness to the document. But it could have just as readily, and much more genuinely, been an open letter rather than a document that mimics the systems of government that have historically enforced the many harmful actions the document evokes (and also those that it does not). This speaks not just to the ALA's inaction but to the many fundamental changes that library systems and librarians working under the guidance of the ALA have not made.

Professor Wayne Wiegand much more powerfully, and humanely, concluded the "Hidden Figures in American Library History" panel with this summary and call to action:

> The stories we just heard are an undeniable part of Southern civil rights and library history. At every event where I've spoken about this topic, there are people in the audience who have stories that few others have heard. These must become part of the profession's collective history. The outcome of desegregation is wonderful, but it is only the first step in the right direction. Young black people today must see that libraries live up to their rhetoric of being free for all.[17]

In 1990, the ALA adopted Policy 61, Library Services for the Poor, ensuring that libraries are "accessible and useful to low-income citizens and to encourage a deeper understanding of poverty's dimensions, its causes, and the ways it can be ended."[18] A few years later, in 1996, members of the Social Responsibilities Round Table of the American Library

Association (SRRT) formed the Hunger, Homelessness, and Poverty Task Force (HHPTF) to promote and implement Policy 61 and to raise awareness of poverty issues.

Some of the stated goals of the HHPTF included:

> Promote removal of all barriers to library and information services, particularly fees and overdue charges.
>
> Promote training opportunities for librarians, in order to teach effective techniques for generating public funding to upgrade library services to poor people.
>
> Promote the incorporation of low-income programs and services into regular library budgets in all types of libraries, rather than the tendency to support these projects solely with "soft money" like private or federal grants.
>
> Promote networking and cooperation between libraries and other agencies, organizations, and advocacy groups in order to develop programs and services that effectively reach poor people.

These are arguably righteous and well-conceived goals, but as of 2021, the ALA includes a note on its website that "to date, the potential of Policy 61 is only partially realized, and much work remains to be done."[19] Although these goals have been outlined for nearly three decades, none of them have been fully met. And, as over 80 percent of public library funding is still local,[20] this still contributes to vast inconsistencies in library quality. Like the segregated libraries of the past, libraries in the poorest communities often have the least funding, inadequate staffing, and the shortest operating hours.

This issue of funding is particularly complicated in the District of Columbia, where the public library is an independent agency of the municipal government, managed by a chief librarian who is selected and reviewed by a Board of Library Trustees. Because it is not overseen by a state budget, the DC Public Library's funding is determined by the Council of the District of Columbia as well as the US Congress. In theory, the nation's capital could have some of the best-funded libraries in the country, providing equal services and support to all. And if equal services and support were not provided, they would—again, in theory—pour the most resources into those branches. But there is ample evidence that this is not the case, and the libraries in the highest-poverty neighborhoods of DC often see the least funding and support. Northwest One is one of these libraries.

As with most institutions in the United States, libraries were founded and funded *by* predominantly White people *for* predominantly White people. The foundational, and still widely accepted, belief that libraries are freedom-granting institutions for all effectively denies and erases the experiences of hundreds of thousands of Americans across centuries. To uphold and uplift this false narrative also allows public libraries to more easily refuse to create fundamental, deep-rooted change. Despite a rich history of people and ideas, and in some cases best intentions that evolved into the modern American public library we now know, racism, xenophobia, and other harmful and sometimes violent forms of exclusion and othering are in the bedrock of public libraries in America and still permeate them today.

In 2017 149,692 librarians in America were White. Only 11,213 were Black, 6,938 were Asian, 4,975 were of two or more races, 1,002 identified as "other," and 545 were American Indian. As of 2020, 89 percent of librarians in leadership or administration roles identify as White and non-Hispanic.[21] With a White majority continually fulfilling roles in libraries and library leadership, other voices are unavoidably lessened, ignored, and lost.

April Hathcock, a Black librarian based in New York City, wrote in a blog post in February 2019: "It seems I will never be able to attend an American Library Association meeting without encountering some kind of racist, sexist trauma. ALA just isn't a safe space in our profession for me. And I'm not the only one."[22] Hathcock went on to describe being harassed and bullied by a White male attendee and by multiple White colleagues. After making a formal complaint to the ALA, she was contacted by its legal representatives and warned against posting about the incident on social media as she "might be held liable if anything happened to the man who confronted her," a response she found threatening—and rightly so. Non-White library workers frequently report, and speak to, imbalances in power within their library systems and prejudice and racism against them by patrons, coworkers, and superiors.

Over two hundred years of public library history tell us many things about the institution's current state, but two especially stand out. The first is that there is a clear and blaring need for more transparency, reckoning, and improvement not only within the field of librarianship but also in our collective understanding of public libraries and librarians' roles in society. The second is that while public libraries are often lauded as social equalizers and the last bastions of democracy, these affectionate understandings are incomplete in ways that allow for continued harm.

Systemic change is slowly happening within libraries and the field of librarianship in large part through conversations and comings together on social media, as well as the activism of librarians and a wider understanding overall of a more nuanced and truthful American history. But there is still a foundational death grip on maintaining racism and segregation within American public spaces in general that certainly does not exclude libraries.

I know I am not alone within the field in having had insufficient knowledge of the past of the public library while actively working in one. If I had had a broader understanding of the history of American libraries at the outset of my career, I would perhaps not have been so surprised by the inequalities, and resulting actions, emotions, and implications of it, that I saw during the seven collective years I worked for the DC Public Schools and the DC Public Library. I would not, perhaps, have been as incredulous and overwhelmed, either. This is the gift of an honest reckoning with our past: freedom to move forward, with truth, in truth. However painful it may be, in the collective or individual process, we eventually come to better and more completely understand the world around us and how we might do better.

The question of who libraries are for, and who they exclude, should not remain cloaked in half-histories and half-truths. This cover—this shield—is imposed by what I had long thought of as "half-truth histories" before encountering famed American historian John Hingham's work on *consensus history*, a term that embodies a pattern of obscuring diversity and conflict in the American past in a smug and self-congratulatory way. At an individual level—when we decide to avoid or lessen the process of seeking broader and more accurate understandings of our history, preferring the ease of a shallow depth over the truth of a deep one—everyone around us is susceptible to our opacity. Consensus history upheld at an institutional level is shattering. As Maria Tumarkin writes in her 2018 book *Axiomatic*, "Time as a straight line is a monstrosity. Sometimes though what's being repeated is hope's absence."[23] We might consider the antidote to consensus history to be raw, honest reckoning. And while this can take centuries for institutions and a lifetime for individuals, both can begin the work of filling hope's absence at any moment. What that might look like in practice demands our consideration.

3

SO, WHAT DO YOU DO?

I was raised in America. All value lies in the future, in the dream, in production. There is no present tense. There is no value in what is, only in what might be made or exploited from what already exists.

—Eve Ensler

IF I SHRINK MYSELF DOWN TO FOUR-YEAR-OLD SIZE, I still remember that being in a library space felt like wandering through a warm tunnel filled with my favorite things in all directions. I was insulated and safe, cushioned by books and quiet. The children's section at my childhood library had a dozen bookcases arranged into three enclaves I could freely wander between, running my hands along the spines, and the quiet of the library created a sort of echo chamber with only the calming reverberations of the drinking fountain and the central air or heating softly humming. The library was more than my favorite place; it was my first beloved destination, first embodied *center*, and it was absolutely sacred. Time at the local library felt open, unending, and certainly special. I have returned to my early library memories many times over the years when I need something comforting and easy to hold in my mind, like a soothing balm I can apply to anything, everything.

That first library of mine was on Main Street in the Village of Williamsville, an upper-middle-class suburb of Buffalo, New York, and it was a five-minute walk from where we lived. At the time, my father worked as a sexton for an Episcopalian church, and the main compensation for his work was our house. Though we lived at the poverty line, the house was huge and welcoming and one of the oldest and most beautiful homes in the village—the type of home people slow down at when they drive past, admiring its size and clear history. Even now, whenever I go home to Buffalo for the holidays, I drop a few miles below the speed limit as I near it. It still, in some small way, feels like my home. I loved it that much.

When he was hired in 1980, my father's annual salary was $3,600, and by 1985, the year I was born, it had risen only slightly, to $4,800. My parents stretched the small income, and our basic needs were always met, but there wasn't money for anything extra.

During the day, my father worked long hours on the upkeep of the church and the many parish buildings while my mother stayed home with me and my two older brothers. At night, our father sometimes stayed at the church late to clean up after events or to dig burial plots in the church cemetery, ensuring that the cremated remains stayed below the frost line throughout Buffalo's many months of winter. A favorite activity, or the one that brought me most comfort when I was three and four, was tucking myself into my bedroom window to watch for him to exit the church after dark, locking the huge oak double doors behind him.

Like most children of the late 1980s, my brothers and I spent much of our time outside, western New York weather permitting, or playing with our toys in the sunroom together. My earliest memories are of creating games with them and running or riding our bikes around the neighborhood with a level of freedom and safety that the decade and neighborhood allowed for. I could often be found reading books in a pile of blankets somewhere. My parents encouraged my reading, and the librarians at the library never told me I could not check out certain books because they were too easy or too hard.

The greatest gift of the library in my earliest years—the gift that so many artists and politicians and doctors and lawyers and poets have cited for centuries all over the world—was the escape that books provided. I could disappear into the lives and adventures of George and Martha, Frog and Toad, Mr. Men and Little Miss, and later, I devoured series—Little House, the Boxcar Children, the Borrowers, Wayside School, Goosebumps, and the Sweet Valley Twins. I could borrow and mine the lives and adventures of others, experiencing life in other centuries, other countries, other worlds. It didn't matter what I had, or did not have, when I was reading. The library was not just a place that functioned outside of economic class—it was where I got to choose my own interests outside my brothers' Star Wars and Indiana Jones that dominated the soundtrack and playtime of our house.

I never considered that library books were shared, that they did not belong to me; I was just happy to read them. Unlike so much other entertainment, books from the library were not constrained by money. Reading as much as I wanted was nothing less than total magic, and libraries provided so much of it. This was my earliest understanding of public libraries. By my small-person understanding, they made life infinitely better.

In the spring of 1989, the minister of the church where my father worked hammered wooden stakes in a straight line down the middle of our backyard and tied one long red string across them. Father Gary relied on my father for any physical labor, so no one was as surprised to see the shoddy barrier he constructed as my father was. Father Gary told my parents he put up the string because he didn't want our two cats to come near the rectory where he lived on the other side of our home. He had his own yard there, contained by a white picket fence. The space in between the two houses—all open grass—had been mine and my brothers' favorite outside area to play in. The red line allotted us a significantly smaller piece of it. My brothers and I could not understand this new parameter, especially since Father Gary's own children were grown adults and none of them lived at home. We continued to play outside, but we missed having full access to the yard.

We were a watchful and protective team of three outside, dealing with cuts, bee stings, slivers, and neighborhood bullies, and we knew to band together when necessary. Father Gary was a favorite target of our sibling comradery, and the red line was his worst transgression yet. We retaliated by uprooting his prized garden flowers. My small arms fit through the white slats of Father Gary's fence with ease, and I can still remember exactly how good it felt to rip up and back, passing decapitated daffodils and tulips to a brother who'd take turns running and hiding them in a storage shed that held the mower our father used to mow both sides of the yard. We were soon caught for the flowers but had other ammunition. We spent days collecting sticks and forming balls of mud around their ends. If we added a little water from the spigot on the side of our house to the dried mud and aimed hard enough, our concoctions stuck to most surfaces and hardened there again in the sun. Once we had tested their effectiveness and created a small arsenal, we lined up and hurled them at the side of Father Gary's house, careful to aim for areas that were not draped in ivy. It required a ladder and a paint scraper to pry them from the sides of the second floor once they were finally discovered, but by then, we could more easily deny that we were the culprits.

My brothers and I understood the judgment being passed on us. If we were going to be labeled "bad" by others, regardless of how we behaved, we might as well enjoy upholding the label. Father Gary, a White, upper-middle-class priest, was my first lived example of someone who wielded his power unkindly against people he thought of as less-than. In an additional knock, he had started to request that my father stay out of sight of the parishioners. At a rare church service my mother attended, she overheard a seated parishioner hiss, "They fuck like rabbits" as she passed by, carrying me in her arms. Father Gary had his own three children, but it was our small family who was equated with rabbits, with being wild and lascivious.

That summer, just before I entered kindergarten, we moved out of the house on South Cayuga Road. The church had ended its sexton program, and we lost residence of the house as my father lost his job. My mother was less than a year back to working as a special education teacher and though her salary was higher than my father's, there hadn't been time to save. Determined to keep us in the Williamsville school system—regularly rated one of the best in western New York—they got a loan for a small ranch house a mile away from the house on S. Cayuga. In our new, smaller home, it was easier to hear conversations and arguments about money. I grew up learning how to save, scrimp, budget, compartmentalize. If food had mold on it, we scraped it off and ate the "good" parts (something I still do, to the horror of some friends and romantic partners). Our showers were timed—three minutes each—and we could expect a loud bang from near the showerhead the second the microwave timer went off, our mother's knuckle rapping on the back of a kitchen cupboard on the other side of the wall. The thermostat in winter went up to sixty-eight degrees, maximum, and if any of us tried to lift it a little higher, even on the subzero days with frostbite warnings, even when the snow was so high it came up to the windows, an argument erupted. Very few of my friends visited our house after middle school—by then the furniture my parents bought when we moved in was fraying, the brown carpet was worn and flattened, and there was a hole in our bathroom floor where the wood had rotted. I was embarrassed. It's painful to remember these things, even now, more than two decades later, but I understand more fully now how hard my parents worked and how much they did provide for us, which was so much more than what they themselves had had growing up in large families. If I am ashamed and embarrassed now, it is only because of the shame and embarrassment I felt back then, but this is the summation of youth: understanding only in hindsight.

I learned to equate activism with "giving to others" early on. If you didn't have money to give, you gave your kindness, energy, and time. If you *did* have any "extra" money, you were encouraged to give it. This came, in part, from the ideology of the Catholic Church I was raised in—no matter what, we put dollar bills into the passed basket that went down the pews and was filled and emptied, filled and emptied, as it went from parishioner to parishioner—but also from the examples set by my family. Both of my parents had eight siblings apiece and all had been raised to help others in similar ways.

Before I understood basic math or spelling or social skills, I understood that money determined most of the ease our family did and did not have. I also understood that if I wanted to get ahead, if I wanted to be able to get more than I gave, I had to make money of my own. There is a net that financial security provides, and for some people, the sun always rises, the utilities are always on, and you call exterminators and plumbers if you need them. For most of my friends, money had always been there, quietly working in the background, but money was loud in my family. I heard it constantly. When I was fourteen, I got my first job at the local mall rolling pretzels at Auntie Anne's pretzel company for minimum wage—$5.15 in 2001. I got a second job at Old Navy and a third at American Eagle the year after. I collected my small paychecks every two weeks and deposited them into my first checking account, proud of myself but also aware that I still did not have what most of my peers had. Not even close.

The same year I started working at the mall, I started shoplifting from it. I took what I thought would make me seem more "normal" in the social hierarchy of high school—a t-shirt or a skirt from Gap or Express, a bottle of body spray from Bath & Body Works, bumper stickers from Spencer's. I was transfixed by the social divides of middle and high school that were determined by wealth and which neighborhood you lived in, and I developed a level of self-consciousness about what I had and did not have that impacted what I gave my time and energy to. This is my story, but it is so many other people's story too, though as I was growing up, it often felt like it was only mine.

Everything from my childhood influenced my decision to become a librarian; I just did not see it at the time. I don't remember thinking much in high school about what job I might have as an adult, and I hadn't thought to bring these kinds of questions to my parents. I had been raised to be self-sufficient, and what I could figure out on my own, I figured out on my own. More existential questions like "What do I want out of life and how might I get there?" were ones I asked, but I wasn't sure how to go about answering them.

Shortly after I turned eighteen, I was finally caught and arrested for shoplifting from a grocery store. When I explained my history of stealing and this eventual arrest to a therapist many years later, she gently told me that my actions had been a coping mechanism. "You were doing your best to take care of yourself," she elaborated. I lay on her soft white couch and nodded. The explanation instantly eased years of shame I had carried around with me. My DC government insurance covered these twice-weekly, $150-per-visit sessions. It wasn't until several years later that I considered who gets to hear these things—who can afford to have access to mental health providers who might provide this clarity and who cannot. Who gets to "make mistakes" and who is told that their attempts to meet their needs are unforgivable. Who begins a criminal record that haunts their path forward and who receives probation that clears their criminal record upon completion, as I did. I was able to sign up for a credit card with no problem and charge my lawyer to it, and I did not have to report the arrest to the university I ended up attending. My life continued where so many other people's lives have been stopped. I didn't know it then, but this was an additional piece of an overarching question I would spend most of early adulthood trying to answer: how could there be so much inequality?

I was in a relationship with a similarly pathless man named Chad during these years. Chad was handsome and charming when he wanted to be, but he could also be cruel and demeaning. When we were in public, he'd sometimes lean into my ear, flashing a smile at friends looking on, and start to whisper, "What you just said was so stupid. Aren't you an English major? Aren't you supposed to be smart?" The smile on his face made the moment look sweet to outsiders, but his voice was an unkind hiss. Chad had dropped out of college before we met, and I was encouraging him to go back and finish his BA in psychology. He had inherited a sum of money from an accident and another from a family member and had been blowing it on booze and whatever else he felt like for years. The money was finally dwindling, and he needed a plan B. Determined as ever to help, I filled out application materials for him to reapply to college and carried them around in a brown leather messenger bag I'd spent months saving up for. The bag eventually became stretched and heavy with all the application materials, and the side I carried the bag on visibly lowered my right shoulder when I traveled between our two apartments. At some point, the metaphor finally landed, but still, I did not break up with him.

Chad was part of the life I thought I was supposed to have, one where I stayed near family in Buffalo, got a job I felt neutral about to pay my bills, got married, and, as a final step, bought a house and had children. It was what some of my friends were starting to do and what most of my older cousins had already done. I wish I could remember the rearrangement of things—if it was one moment or several, if it was something someone said or something I read—that caused my first major internal shift, but I began to realize I wanted much more. A boyfriend who was kind to me or no boyfriend at all. A job that did not have such late hours and did not require me to wear a uniform and insole-lined black shoes that smelled so bad I put them in my freezer between shifts because I could not afford to buy new ones. I wanted to be excited to tell people what I did for work. I wanted to have enough money to start doing and seeing more places, more things. I wanted more than what I had.

It took only one person showing me a graph with the average salary of a librarian to make me decide I wanted to do that. The number, in my memory, was around $38,000. I didn't quite know what being a librarian meant, but I knew I loved books and liked helping people, and that those were surely essential parts of the job. I applied to graduate school and was accepted to the MLS program at UB. Chad, for his part, never submitted the application materials I created for him. He needed only to request letters of recommendation, and even though I had drafted the e-mails for him, he never sent them. Finally, in the summer before I started grad school, I broke up with him.

No part of me consciously understood the interwoven pieces of my life that led to my decision at the time to become a librarian. How being raised to help others, above all else, had led me to a helping career. How a fear of continued, lifelong financial struggle trumped any intuitive feeling I had about who I was and what I might enjoy and be good at. How a lifelong feeling of being less-than had left me desperate to please others. It was only once I was a librarian that I began to untangle this internal knot I had created. It would be more years, still, before I learned to identify similar knots in others, and an entire decade before I began to understand what, and who, perpetuates these knots.

I entered the master's in library science program at the University at Buffalo (UB) in the winter of 2009. My area of focus was school libraries, but I took general courses that also qualified me to be a public, academic, or special librarian. Two six-week teaching practicums were required for the school librarian track, and I completed the first at a middle school in the same school district I had attended. The library there was massive, with a full-time librarian who was a beloved fixture of the school community, as well as two part-time library associates. The students were predominantly White, upper middle class, and intimately familiar to me. I knew almost immediately after I started that I did not want to put my skills and energy into working with students who would inevitably have the best possible resources no matter who their librarian was. I petitioned to temporarily move from Buffalo to New York City to complete my second and final required six-week practicum there, and the university approved it.

The position I accepted was in the library of a combined public elementary and middle school located directly across the street from the studio housing *The Wendy Williams Show*. As students lined up outside the school gates in the morning, people who hoped to be audience members for that day's taping did the same. New York City was full of an energy I never felt in Buffalo, and I loved everything about it, down to my forty-minute morning commute from a friend's place where I was crashing in Greenpoint and the bagel stand I stopped at most mornings. My supervising librarian, Debbie, was the only negative part of my New York City experience. A former screenwriter and costume designer, she privately called the students assholes and complained to me about nearly every aspect of the job. During scheduled class library time, she mostly read out loud to students from chapter books while they colored with crayons on printer paper, regardless of their grade level. My training at the library consisted of standing in for these read-alouds, where Debbie was miffed to see students listening carefully when I read using different voices, acting out some of the characters' actions as I walked around the room, pausing to praise their drawings. It was the bare minimum I could imagine doing. The students liked me and I liked them and I vowed to do and be better than Debbie when I became a librarian. I even wondered if the principal would offer me Debbie's job at the end of the year, but by summer there was a hiring freeze in all New York City public schools. Worried about finding a job, I applied to school librarian positions all across the country: Los Angeles, DC, Detroit, Boston, and Chicago. I was willing to go to any city that would hire me.

The only place to give me an interview was the DC Public Schools, and so in June of 2011, six months after graduating with my MLS degree, I moved into my brother's rented condo in Northwest DC. He had moved to the area five years earlier to begin his career as a social worker. By July, I had accepted a position at Thomson Elementary School, a Title I school less than a mile from the White House.

It was and is a joke among DC residents that people ask what you "do for work" early on in conversations to see who and what you know and who and what you might be connected to. It's usually a quick assessment to see how much attention and time they should give you more than it is any real interest in what you do. During my first months in DC, I was not aware of this social custom and was shocked by the things people said when I told them I was a librarian. One of the most memorable responses came from someone dressed as the Brawny paper towel man at a Halloween party that first fall. He and his mustache had looked down at me and laughed for a full thirty seconds when I said I was a children's librarian.

When he was done laughing, he said, "Oh yeah, what's a typical day? You read a bunch of books with kids on your lap?"

I had spent any free time I had that summer setting up Thomson's library with reading nooks, freshly washed stuffed animals from thrift stores, colorful puzzles with corresponding books, and Jenga blocks I'd neatly labeled with sight words so students could play the game and practice their reading. I'd worked full-time all summer at a DC chain restaurant trying to save as much money as I could before my first paycheck from the school came in. I quit the restaurant a few days before school started and moved into my own small English basement apartment in the Woodley Park neighborhood of Northwest DC. There was one window in the entire place, located in the bathroom, and by winter I would discover there was a rat infestation in the walls that my landlord insisted was just the heat turning on. It was a three-minute walk to the Red Line, and my rent was $1,300 per month—the equivalent, I learned, of one of my biweekly paychecks.

The library I inherited was a mess. In addition to the collection being largely out of order, it had also not been properly weeded in over sixty years, and many of the resources were outdated and damaged. Books on the shelves were about countries that had dissolved, planets that were no longer planets, and several were about *someday* landing on the moon. There wasn't enough time to fix this, or even make a dent in fixing it, before the school year began and certainly not once it was underway. On my first day with students, two of my five classes came in running and yelling, refusing to sit in the seats I had carefully created neat seating charts for, no matter how I asked. I quickly realized that my time spent perfecting Word Jenga would have been better used reading some—*any*—literature about managing a classroom.

The seasoned teachers' classes arrived in single-file lines and went to their assigned seats quietly, but quickly lost attention and interest as the lessons I planned took up only fifteen minutes of the forty-five we had together. I had misjudged everything. During my final class of the day, a first grader with his forearm in a cast wound his arm up in small circles and smacked me as hard as he could with it. It was a red cast, his name was Malachi, and I cried in my office the moment he and his classmates left. I eventually walked down to Malachi's first grade classroom and found his young teacher in a similar state. Later, we would both come to learn that Malachi's home life was difficult and that he, as well as his single mother, had multiple learning disabilities. Malachi's mom adored and loved him, but she often relied on physical punishment to manage his behavior. His teachers, including me, struggled to find ways to reach him when he ran circles around the room, hit other students, and burst into crying fits that sometimes lasted most of the school day. In an IEP meeting his mother gave permission to everyone present to "smack him," and the guidance counselor gently explained that this was not something any of us could, or would, do. I made every effort to earn Malachi's trust rather than his "good" behavior, and I was mostly successful. By winter break, Malachi ran in for a hug whenever he saw me.

Memories of Malachi are some of the few I recall clearly from my first year as a librarian. Most first-year educators will tell you similar things: they vaguely remember the feelings of deep failure mixed with sporadic and minimal success, but the students who affected them the most stay with them forever. There was also Amelia, a soft-spoken and sweet third grader with huge brown eyes and her little brother, Angelo, who was not soft spoken at all. That winter, Angelo's kindergarten teacher discovered that his father had been putting him inside of a turned-off oven when he got to be "too much." By spring Angelo had been diagnosed with ADHD, and his father was in prison for something unrelated to the abuse. Angelo struggled to follow classroom routines, but loved to play basketball, so I would end some days in the gym with him and a teacher friend, aiming basketballs at the hoops.

There was Mateo, a kindergartner who tried to charge his body into his thirty classmates during story time every few weeks. Each time, I opened my arms wide to catch him, and he softened his body just before contact. I'd hold him in one of those hugs and keep reading.

There was Owen, a third grader whose arms were covered in grease burns from manning the fryer at his family's nearby Chinatown restaurant after school most days, often late into the night. His little brother was in the school's Head Start program and sometimes couldn't sit on the library floor for story time because his bottom was so raw from being hit by the grandmother who looked after them most of the time. Both boys wanted to do well and be accepted, but their behavior scared other students. They had violent outbursts, and Owen especially would sometimes scratch and scream at people. He spoke Mandarin Chinese at home, as more than half the students at Thomson did, but he also knew an impressive amount of English curse words and could string them together in ways that I was privately amused by. In the spring of that first year, Owen was admitted to the children's psychiatric ward at Children's National Hospital for several days. His teacher and I rode our bikes to the hospital, but we were not permitted inside to visit him.

Many of my students at Thomson struggled with their mental health, and many of them had experienced more pain, loss, and trauma in their young lives than most adults in the building could comprehend. We received some information from IEP meetings, but much of our understanding developed by witnessing various incidents, behaviors, and physical marks (and reporting them to Child Protective Services). But there was no way to truly understand what some of our students had been through or were still going through. On several occasions, I was the only thing between a kindergartner named Sharma and his attempts to throw himself over a railing and down three flights of school stairs. I was also the aching palm between the banging forehead of a second grader and a thick wall of glass as he screamed, "I want to die!" over and over. I spent many, if not most, of my lunch breaks that first year with a second grader named Marisol, teaching her how to calm her body with simple yoga poses, letting her read out loud to me, and telling her, "No, of course you don't scare me" when she softly spoke about wanting to hurt her teachers or classmates.

I always sat with my students—on the floor, in corners, on top of tables, in stairwells. I put my body near theirs and repeated the same thing: "Whatever you do or say, I'm not going to leave you." This was the best way I found to prove myself to be a safe person for my students: letting them know I would stick it—whatever *it* was—out with them. I acknowledged and sat with them and their pain. It was pain I could relate to sometimes, but often I could only begin to fathom what, and who, had hurt them so much.

No one had taught me to do any of this, and I did not know if it was best practice or what my students—most of them Hispanic, Latino, Black, and Asian—needed. No part of any teaching training had prepared me for how much my students needed, so I relied on what I knew from my own experiences. I began to build my pedagogy around caring for the child first and the learning second. I was able to do this, in part, because my role in the school community as a librarian was not tied to standardized test scores. They could "fail" at using the library, and it didn't impact a grade or my paycheck.

I was hired at Thomson just after the *Waiting for "Superman"* documentary came out and Michelle Rhee had resigned as the school district's chancellor. Rhee left in her wake IMPACT, the unpopular teacher effectiveness rating system tied to standardized test scores. Teachers delivering low test scores could be demoted or fired at the end of the year. These and other expectations for teachers were nonsensical given the challenges many of their students, and families, faced outside of the school environment. Additionally, DCPS was trying out a new curriculum every, or every other, year. Just as I often felt that my students were set up for failure, so too were their teachers. Being the school's librarian gave me a unique perspective as I saw and knew every single student in the building and many of their family members. I had never worked in an environment that so blatantly called for me to look at the world around me and notice the pains and disparities that permeated my students', and their families', lives. It was one thing to have spent childhood near the poverty line as a White person in a well-resourced school district; it was an entirely different thing to grow up as a poor Black or Mandarin Chinese or Hispanic child in a metropolis with a public school system regularly recognized as one of the worst in the country.

Feelings of helplessness and hopelessness permeated my first year of teaching. Within the walls of Thomson, there was a daily barrage of trauma and anger and pain, and I was often exhausted by trying to process it all. Back then I did not know the term *white saviorism*, nor did I consider myself to be participating in it. No part of me thought I was uniquely capable of helping or teaching or leading because I was White. I had taken the job because it was the only one I had been offered from the urban school systems I applied to. I knew full well that I could not "save" any of my students, even when I called Child Protective Services as a mandated reporter, even when I came early and stayed late. What I could do was be kind and try to develop their curiosities and interests. I could create a safe and loving space, surrounded by books, and mostly I succeeded, though I am certain my own implicit biases, and naïveté, impacted how I showed up to the community. I did my best with what I had, how and where I had been raised, and who I had become as an adult.

When I arrived in DC in 2011, I was twenty-four years old. Thomson was near the DC epicenter of the Occupy Wall Street protests, and I heard the daily chants of "We! Are! The 99 percent!" whenever I went for a walk on my lunch break. I had no understanding that a small number of billionaires owned the majority of America's wealth, in part because I was young and naive, but also because the American economy had shifted drastically between 1980 and 2010. Technological advances combined with late twentieth-century deregulation and deindustrialization created something like a second Gilded Age, with changes that I was too young to fully understand while still in grade school and too young and perhaps self-absorbed to realize in the first years of college. I was stunned by the Occupy protesters' tents and their willingness to sleep outside in a busy area of the District. At the time my dominant thought was, *Do these people just . . . not want to work?* My understanding of the movement was informed by my own upbringing—that you worked, no matter what—but it was obviously vague. I was not actively opposed to or in disagreement with Occupy, but I also did not fully comprehend what they were trying to achieve. It misaligned with my core understanding of work as not just a financial necessity, but as an important sense of identity and life purpose.

I now understand that the identity work gives us is often deeply tied up in a capitalist American culture, and choosing to deeply align with our jobs and job titles as who we are often diminishes or eliminates altogether a meaningful sense of inherent self-worth as human beings. All human beings deserve shelter, food, health care, and safety regardless of their levels of capitalist productivity.

In 2011 I walked around the Occupy protesters and encampment in a similar manner as I walked around houseless people, but I did not make this connection back then. I had empathy and compassion for the houseless people, and yet I did not see how many of the Occupy Wall Street protesters were using their time, bodies, and energy to fight for themselves and also other marginalized groups. Beyond being an active protest, Occupy was about forcing people to see the cost of immense wealth in human form, in the way that the protesters made themselves so visible. I had not considered the one percent because I was just trying to exist in the social class I was in; I was just hoping to get one rung higher on that ladder. I put my energies there, through work.

In DC I began to understand the distinctions between social classes more clearly—that ideas of charity, community care, and mutual aid were intimately tied to race, religion, and other determining factors of socioeconomic status. I knew how I felt about my own experience growing up with less than most of my peers, but I had not critically considered why it was this way or how it was worse for many, many others. Poet, activist, and writer Sonya Renee Taylor speaks about these distinctions of class as a hierarchy of bodies. There are some who will never get to the top, or anywhere near it, but that will not stop them from devoting their lives to getting one or two rungs higher.

I had watched most of my large extended family engage in this ladder climbing across generations. My paternal grandfather and his three brothers started a landscaping company called Oliver Brothers' Landscaping in 1953 that permanently changed our family name from the Italian *Olivieri* to a more Americanized *Oliver*, a change made in hopes of increasing their chances of being hired at a time when Italians were often passed up for jobs. In 1963 my father and his twin brother started to work full-time for the company, and its name changed again to Oliver & Sons Landscaping. All the six sons in the family worked for the company at some point, and as my grandfather's retirement neared, they went on to work as laborers, customer service associates, and custodians. The two sisters found office support work. None of the siblings ever received college degrees, and my eldest brother was the first of the ten nieces or nephews on that side of the family to get a college degree. My other brother was next and then me.

My maternal grandmother worked as a registered nurse, and my maternal grandfather as an electronics technician, a trade he learned from his father at age fourteen. My maternal grandparents also had eight children, and they emphasized to each of them the importance of receiving a higher education. In a beautiful letter my grandfather gave to my grandmother on their fiftieth wedding anniversary, he wrote:

> There has been richer and poorer. The richer hasn't been that rich and though it didn't seem to be the case at the time, maybe we weren't _that_ poor. I sometimes have thought that we may have done our many children a favor by being poor when they were young. I am very proud of them for earning their educations on their own, with so little help from us. They are self-reliant, resourceful people who deserve not only our love but also our deepest respect.

I love this letter. I keep it folded inside of a favorite book and go to it when I want a succinct reminder of what, and who, I come from. And I agree with it—my many maternal aunts and uncles are intelligent and accomplished individuals, and most of them went on to college and became firefighters, nurse practitioners, professors, and educators, often climbing the ranks to leadership positions. They are caring, considerate people who give back, my mother included. But the letter also serves as a reminder to me that the lower you are on the socioeconomic ladder, the more your moral character is dependent on your work ethic and how productive you can be.

Our country has long equated _money_ with intelligence, power, and strength, and _poverty_ with weakness, incompetence, and mediocrity. And yet folks in "lower" socioeconomic groups have deep-rooted resourcefulness, cleverness, empathy, loyalty, and quick-thinking skills that wealthier people don't have the same _need_ to develop to survive. While these skills are enviable and valuable ones, especially as our world shifts to a need for more resourcefulness, ingenuity, and physical labor, they often develop from immense struggle. Wealthy people develop them differently, in more controlled and comfortable ways: through higher education, wellness classes, TED Talks, and similar. They do this in the comfort of their own spaces and rarely, if ever, out of any necessity. I saw these and similar, more overarching understandings begin to come to a head after I moved to DC, and they became more and more frustrating and heartbreaking as I continued working in a Title I school environment.

At the end of my second year at Thomson, my position was reduced to half-time for the coming school year. Libraries were, and are still, a common first cut from budgets in DCPS, and I was not particularly surprised by the decision. I tried to make the part-time salary work for the fall and winter of that third school year, but it was not enough. I was in a long-distance relationship and decided to move to my partner's home on the west coast of Canada instead of trying to afford DC on my own. Just before the school's winter break in 2013, I left Thomson and moved to a small town on Vancouver Island.

I have never felt as rich as I did when I lived on the island. Not monetarily wealthy, certainly, but in spirit. We lived in a small one-bedroom apartment midway up the island in the city of Nanaimo, close to where Nigel, my partner, worked. Money was tight—we shared a car that eventually broke down, and I could not legally work in Canada as an American— but still, we had this good thing. We had each other. Nigel was the kindest partner I had ever had in adult life, and he helped allow for my weekdays to be filled with writing and long walks around lakes and through dense forest. On weekends, we explored the beautiful home Nigel had grown up in; there were walks down hidden logging roads to secluded mountain streams, visits to the slow coastal towns of Ucluelet and Tofino, and meals and gatherings in the capital city of Victoria. My many quiet days in nature and seclusion were peaceful and relaxing, but eventually I felt something akin to what I had felt years earlier in Buffalo before I entered my MLS program: I wanted more. A year and a half in, my relationship with Nigel no longer felt symbiotic or sustainable. I wanted to leave the island and live somewhere busier for a few years, and he wanted to stay. He refused my suggestion that we move to nearby Seattle where we could both more readily find work and community. The partner I had valued for his sense of adventure did not, I realized, seek unfamiliar adventure away from his island. No matter how much I had started to love the island, no matter how much I loved this person, I knew in my gut that I could not settle down for life in one place just yet.

Nigel stayed on his quiet island, and I returned to my busy city. A ferry and two airplanes put thousands of miles between us again, and I knew I would never run into him on a random city sidewalk or in my search for the bathroom at a party. I knew I would very likely never see him again, period. I was decided but also crushed. I had left for good in the spring. A few months later, I visited my doctor for the first time in nearly two years, and we were both in awe when he discovered I had developed an irregular heartbeat. In my interpretation, my heart had quite literally broken. I had assumed this physical symptom was another side effect of the relationship ending, but I was also aware that a persistent weight I had felt on my chest for months lifted the moment I touched back down on the East Coast. I was back where things made sense. Where my role in the community made sense.

There is a seriousness to DC that can feel maddening to outsiders and soothing to residents. I missed the rhythm and hum of it all: the pace locals kept in the Metro, dodging tourists and yelling "Excuse me!" at people not keeping to the right on the escalators; running errands without small talk from the cashier; the dizzying effect of people exercising all throughout the city after work, maneuvering around pedestrians and cars as they ran off work stress and I tried to make it to museums before closing time. People know how to be alone and how to leave others alone in DC, and I missed the relief of it all. Being back in DC felt not just familiar and comforting, but like being able to breathe at full capacity again. Where I had expected a calmer life closer to nature to slow me down, it was in the fast pace of a city that I could really stop and catch my breath. The ease of life on the island had been too much for me. It felt complicit, somehow, all that comfort knowing the world I had left behind. And so I returned to working as a librarian in the DC Public Schools, this time in the wealthy Georgetown neighborhood.

———————

Students who lived in the Georgetown neighborhood walked or scootered a short distance down cobblestone streets to the wrought-iron school gates of Hyde-Addison Elementary School. A huge cherry blossom tree shaded the sprawling school playground, and a family of ducks frequented the school's garden. John Kerry lived just up the street, and I became familiar with the Secret Service agents who sat outside his home. I'd pass them on my walk to grab coffee, one in the driver's seat and one in the passenger seat, and we'd share a smile and nod.

Hyde-Addison was one of the oldest schools in DC, tucked away in one of its richest neighborhoods, and the staff were mostly White. When I started there in 2015, people like NPR host Guy Raz still had their children enrolled. Many parents prided themselves on keeping their children in the public schools, but when more and more "lottery students"—predominantly students of color—started to enroll, families, mostly White families, increasingly opted to put their children in private schools. Raz pulled his two boys out by November of my first year and as a parting gift hosted a live interview with journalist and author Amanda Ripley about her book *The Smartest Kids in the World: And How They Got That Way*. Proceeds from the ticket sales went directly to the school.

Ripley's book analyzes and compares the American education system to international education systems, focusing on three American high school students who studied for a year in Finland, South Korea, and Poland. The book is written largely in critique of the American public education system. It occurred to me that this might have been Raz's way of explaining, or defending, his decision to pull his children from Hyde-Addison, but the truth was most families who live in the Georgetown neighborhood can afford to send their children to expensive private schools, and they do. Fewer options exist for parents and children in lower-income neighborhoods. As I listened to Ripley and Raz talk about how other countries were educating their children better,

I thought about some of my students at Hyde-Addison—the students who got up hours before school to catch multiple buses and trains to make it on time, often arriving at school already exhausted and hungry. I had ideas of what it meant to give them a so-called better education and so did Ripley, Raz, and presumably many of the parents in attendance. Ripley and Raz had both made careers out of conjecture around such ideas. But these ideas were perpetually distant from the lived experiences of these students and their families and the very real limitations they faced.

Students who wanted to attend a DC public school other than the one assigned to them by their home address had to enter the citywide lottery, languishing on waiting lists for months and sometimes years. In one attempt to keep the lists more fair, former DCPS chancellor Antwan Wilson wrote a 2016 rule with Mayor Muriel Bowser that banned special transfers for the family members of government officials. Three months after it was signed, Wilson broke his own rule to transfer his daughter from Duke Ellington School of the Arts to Wilson High. Wilson had a waiting list of over six hundred students, and the chancellor's daughter skipped over all of them. In the days before his forced resignation, Wilson claimed that he had acted as a father seeking what was best for his daughter, citing "tunnel vision" because his daughter was having social and emotional issues at her current school.[1] Parents in the school system rightly argued that they wanted the exact same treatment for their own children. (A simple Google search shows that this is only one of thousands of examples of unequal access to quality public education in the District.)

The typical time for neighborhood parents at Hyde-Addison to pull their children out and put them in private schools was the first or second grade. The upper-grade classrooms were made up of much higher percentages of students of color from high-poverty neighborhoods who were attending school through the lottery system. I had heard classroom teachers explain many times that "they pull them out before the upper grades. Things are still pretty okay when they're younger, but not in the later grades." *They* were the wealthy, mostly White, parents.

Beyond my frustration with the many disparities that the school embodied, I had never seen eye to eye with the principal at Hyde-Addison.

Principal Newman visited the library while I had students exactly three times in the three school years I worked there, and each visit was brief. The one instance where she stayed for more than a few minutes was to speak to a class of fourth graders who had been particularly tough that year. Many of the students yelled, cursed, fought, and threw things at each other and, sometimes, at their teachers. I had struggled to find a behavior system or set of agreements that worked well for all of us, and Principal Newman was going around to talk to them in all their Specials classrooms where their behavior had been particularly difficult to manage.

When she came that afternoon, Principal Newman gathered the students around the carpet I used for story time, instructed them to "sit crisscross applesauce," and asked them to imagine the last time they saw a horse. I was seated in a chair across from her staring at the backs of my students' heads, deeply grateful they could not see the look on my face. Many of the students who came to the school through the lottery had been born and raised in DC and most, I could guess, had not spent a lot of time around horses. Their confused reactions confirmed this. (There had been a similar conundrum with a state exam in my second year of teaching when a math equation talked about Jose using a lawn mower to mow a certain number of square feet of his lawn. Many students got the question wrong because, as they later explained to their teachers, they did not know what a lawn mower was and thought they might be missing an essential part of the question.)

"Now, picture that horse's blinders," Newman continued.

"Its *what*?"

"You know, its blinders," she repeated, cupping her hands on the sides of her face, pushing back her blowout, to mimic a horse tack. "Think of when you walk up to a horse and see its blinders."

"What do blinders do?"

"They prevent the horse from seeing behind it or to the sides so it doesn't get scared by what's around it."

I was beginning to sense where she was going and felt my mouth open.

"You need to learn how to put on your blinders!" Again, she cupped her hands around her face, her blue eyes open wide. "When some of your classmates start acting in a way you know they shouldn't, you need to put on your blinders!" A few of the students on the carpet placed their own hands on the sides of their faces and started turning their heads to see how much they could and couldn't see around them.

"Good! Don't give them attention when they act up, just ignore it and focus on your job!"

With that, Newman stood up, smoothed her pencil skirt, and walked out of the library with her stiletto heels clicking on the floor, leaving me to answer the students' many follow-up questions. The following week, I started a buddy reading system between the fourth graders and a classroom of Head Start students who were two and three years old. The fourth graders used their library time to select books for themselves and then ones to read to their buddies, who came down to join them in the library. With a task they enjoyed—something I had been trying to find for months—there were much fewer issues. Another teacher and I spent the rest of the year discreetly throwing on our "blinders" at staff meetings as a cue to each other that we thought something being said was out of touch or unhelpful.

Principal Newman appeared to be invested in giving students what she thought of as equal access to opportunity, but the opportunities that she and many of the other wealthier parents wanted for the students reflected what they cared about, not necessarily what was most beneficial to all students. There was a science fair, pet chinchillas, and a partnership with a Smithsonian museum where the point person, on the verge of tears, asked me how in the world I did this—*this* being teaching at Hyde—every day. There was also an annual fundraising gala where neighborhood families donated and auctioned off things like Louis Vuitton suitcases and weekends at second homes while drinking from the open bar. The poorer parents almost never attended.

———

At the end of my second year at Hyde, my position was again reduced to half-time. Instead of leaving the schools or DC, I accepted a second part-time librarian job at another DC public school and began my sixth inconsecutive year as a school librarian split between the two. Garrison

Elementary was in the heart of the U Street Corridor, known for its music, jazz, and nightlife venues like Black Cat, DC9, and the Lincoln Theatre. Upward of 75 percent of the students who attended the school lived at or below the poverty line, qualifying it as a Title I school. I began the year with several new staff members, including the principal. The school district had recently put money into a renovation of Garrison, and there was a brand-new library, with new furniture, books, and carpeting, funded by Target.

Garrison reminded me of Thomson. There was a sense of community and commitment to all types of learners that permeated the decisions, activities, and routines within the school walls. Our student body was diverse and so was the staff. All the people who worked at Garrison were doing their best to collectively work for something better for the students, and we relied on that existing in each other. I was reminded of why I had loved Thomson so much—diverse communities, especially communities that are marginalized and underserved, are often more welcoming, accepting, and warm.

Managing the work at two schools—serving a combined community of nearly five hundred students and over one hundred faculty and staff members—began to take a toll on me, though. I was responsible for teaching thirty forty-five-minute classes per week between the two schools, and there was little time to manage the actual library collection, let alone plan lessons. I was on four committees and had lunch and recess duties at both schools, and the previous year Principal Newman had made me the school testing coordinator for Hyde-Addison. The vice principal and I were responsible for administering the statewide Common Core exams to hundreds of students in addition to continuing to be responsible for most of our normal work. With an understanding of the overwhelming amount of responsibilities the new school year would hold, I had applied and interviewed for a children's librarian position with the DC Public Library that August, but months had gone by with no word. One week before the school's winter break, the DC Public Library e-mailed me with an offer letter. Within a half hour of reading it, I e-mailed both principals my resignation, explaining that I would work through the winter break and a few days after, but that was all I had left to offer.

The public library would be different. I'd have more time, energy, coworkers; more support, more books, more people to serve. There would be no designated class times, no recess or lunch duty, no principal making most of the decisions. Having coworkers who were also librarians, along with the support of library technicians and associates, would make the job—whatever it entailed—easier. I was certain. I let students and families know where they could find me, and I left the DC Public Schools for a final time.

4

THE LIBRARY FROM "L"

A good window lets the outside participate.

—Natalie Diaz, *Postcolonial Love Poem*

MY BRANCH ASSIGNMENT ARRIVED ONE WEEK before my first day on the job as I was sitting on a boulder in Joshua Tree National Park. I had used the two-week space between jobs to take a four-day vacation to California, and in my rock scramble from desert ground to a higher altitude, I'd unknowingly stumbled into cell phone service. The *ding!* startled me out of the solitude and quiet. The subject line read "Northwest One," a branch name I did not recognize, and so I clicked on the address included in the body of the e-mail to see where the library was on a map. I was surprised to see it situated near so many places I recognized and frequented, including a popular breakfast place I sometimes went out of my way to visit for its goat cheese and herb biscuits.

I stopped in at A Baked Joint my first morning at Northwest One, chatting with the staff about the new job. The two young women at the counter were confused.

"There's a library around here?"

"A block and a half that way," I said, motioning to my left.

"Wow, did not know that."

Northwest One was on L Street NW in the small Sursum Corda neighborhood of DC situated across from a Baptist church and attached to Walker-Jones Education Campus, a DC public school serving students from PK3 to eighth grade. The building sat between busy New Jersey Avenue NW and First Street NW, close enough to I-395 to hear a constant whirring of traffic, but far enough away from K Street to be easily overlooked by people who lived, worked, or visited nearby. It was one block east of NPR headquarters and a few minutes' walk to several popular DC restaurants.

Looking at it on a map today, people would identify its location as being in the NoMa neighborhood, but the moniker NoMa was not one that DC residents used regularly until a Metro station by the same name opened in 2004, and it took several more years for it to really catch on. The station was created in large part at the behest of a group of local commercial property owners who saw promise in the neighborhood in the early 2000s. The group formed a business improvement district (BID) in 2007 to foster commercial development around the NoMa-Gallaudet U Metro station, helping to attract tenants like Google, NPR, and the Department of Homeland Security. The NoMa I knew when I moved to DC in 2011 had been one I mostly associated with the Greyhound bus depot I frequented to escape DC for New York City and the spices and tchotchkes I bought from garage door storefronts at the Union Market. A 2012 modernization of Union Market brought even more popular restaurants, bars, and businesses to the area. The NoMa BID website describes the NoMa neighborhood in 2021 as "the hip, smart center of the nation's capital, with free outdoor WiFi, terrific walkability, a slew of transit options, and a lengthy stretch of the Metropolitan Branch Trail."[1]

When I think about gentrification, especially rapid gentrification like this, I think about the loss of the *there there*, a concept first described by Gertrude Stein in *Everybody's Autobiography*. Novelist Tommy Orange gives it brilliant further context: "The place where [Stein had] grown up in Oakland had changed so much, that so much development had happened there, that the there of her childhood, the there there, was gone, there was no there there anymore."[2]

The area immediately surrounding Northwest One embodied the loss of a *there there*. It was bordered by battered and woozy-looking housing projects that had once been referred to as the Sursum Corda projects. In 2014, a fourteen-year-old girl named Jahkema Princess Hansen was murdered in her living room where she was watching television with a twelve-year-old friend. Hansen had been scheduled to testify as a witness to a shooting in the neighborhood. She was shot in the head, torso, and leg, and her friend was wounded. Her home was less than a block from the library.

The murder of Hansen has been cited as the final incident to ensure the closure of the projects. Plans to demolish the housing projects had been in place for years, but in 2018 they remained standing with wooden boards across their fronts, collecting graffiti—statues, of a sort, to a different time and neighborhood. Northwest One opened in 2009 with hopeful ambitions for uplifting the neighborhood. The first community space of its kind in the city, the Walker-Jones Education Campus, Northwest One, and RH Terrell Recreation Center were all connected. Within a few years of opening, the rec center closed due to low use and was absorbed by the school. The block began to quiet down and people—people like me—did not realize it was there. Only a few blocks away, though, cafés, restaurants, luxury apartments, and chain stores thrived.

A week before my first shift, I drove by the library after it was closed. I could see the outside facade was made to look modern: the entire front of it was floor-to-ceiling windows, and it was clearly a newer build than everything around it. It was a small branch, but it seemed tidy and organized when peering through its windows.

———————

My first morning working at Northwest One, there had been an ice fog, and the outside temperature read just above freezing on my car's dashboard when I started to drive south down Georgia Avenue NW, gloved hands holding the cold steering wheel. My apartment in 2018 was in a ten-unit building in the Petworth neighborhood of Northwest DC, and it was heated by four old radiators with no controllable thermostat. My super, a lanky man named Sam who had lived in the neighborhood his entire life, had a small apartment in the basement of the building and either ran cold or had no understanding of how much the heat rose to the floors above him. All winter long, the pipes would bubble to life in the early morning until the air was so hot it felt like I would choke if I didn't open a window. I often left the house carrying my coat, letting the winter air cool me down before layering back up. Not all winters in DC see snow and multiple days of below-freezing temperatures, but 2018 did. In that regard, I was thankful for Sam's upkeep.

My commute to the branch was only fifteen minutes if I could edge my car onto Georgia Avenue and over into the left lane to turn onto a side street. The avenue was often gridlocked by 7:30 AM, and drivers already in the middle of their commute would not easily let others nose in. Over the years, I had gotten better at maneuvering my Honda Civic an inch from other cars and sticking the front of it into the traffic so they couldn't get around me without a collision. It was one small but significant way I had learned to take up space in a city whose population had grown by 100,000 people since I first moved there. The horns and shouts no longer bothered me. DC had become home more than any other place had ever been.

Walking up to Northwest One in the morning light, a half hour before opening on my first day, the building immediately looked less impersonal than it had a week earlier. More than a dozen people were waiting under the fifteen-foot stretch of the building's concrete awning. Each of them had a large blue IKEA bag, black garbage bag, or suitcase next to them, filled with blankets and personal items. Some of the people were rolling up familiar thick gray blankets I recognized from seeing them wrapped around unhoused people in parks throughout the city.

As best I could tell, they were all unhoused, and the building now embodied shelter and refuge. There were circular patches of dead grass from urination, empty beer cans, and the smell of body odor and cigarette smoke. The public school attached to the building was already in session, and I could see a security guard through the windows, a metal accordion fence separating him and his post from the small library lobby.

Some people were still slowly emerging from their sleeping bags in puffs of visible air, and no one talked to anyone. A woman in her sixties with hair matted to the left side of her head hissed a symphony of curse words at nothing anyone else could see. A man in his twenties poured a small bottle of liquor into a quarter-full bottle of red Gatorade, shaking it.

I stood clutching my identification card in one gloved hand like it was not just government permission to be there, but proof I was prepared for this job. The hot coffee and artisanal breakfast sandwich in my other hand suddenly felt not just indulgent but ridiculous. I kept my eyes cast down, wondering if there was a *correct* way to stand there, freshly showered, twenty dollars' worth of food in hand, and keys to my newly leased car in my pocket. I thought back to mornings I had walked by the central library branch and seen groups of people sleeping against the building. I'd always been able to walk past, maybe stopping to give someone a dollar, but mostly just considering, briefly, how hard it must be. Standing there that first morning, I felt complicit in a way I never had before.

A little after 8:30 AM, a man in his early thirties came to the doorway and slammed his arm into the security bar to open it for me.

"Come on in, sorry we left you out there. This door's broken. So's the next one. I'm Chris," he said, extending his hand.

Chris was a morning person. I both aspired to his cheerfulness in general and hated it so early in the morning, but I could tell he meant well and was excited to have a new coworker. As we approached the second door, he explained that if I'd started the day before, we wouldn't have met because he'd been in court. A patron named Ms. Lee was suing him for the third time. He quickly explained that Ms. Lee thought she was responsible for creating a secret café on top of the Spy Museum at the behest of the FBI. She claimed in court documents that when Chris had barred her from the library for six months for throwing the bathroom key with its large plastic keychain at another patron's face, it had prevented her from doing her work. He then said, "Anyway, she's barred for another three months. Welcome to Northwest One!" The security gate on the other side of the second broken door didn't work either.

Next to this final door was a "Does your bag fit?" display like one you'd find at an airport bag check. In large text, it explained that patrons could bring in one large bag so long as it fit into the bin below, without forcing it, plus one personal item. Anything more than that and they couldn't enter without leaving the excess in the hallway. I thought about how all the people waiting outside had their bags protectively pressed against their bodies. I realized this policy meant leaving at least half of their belongings unattended in the lobby.

The library felt even smaller inside than it had looked from the outside. At 4,500 square feet, there were only a few tables in each designated section, a small computer lab, one restroom, and a workroom. It was still clear the library had looked nice when it first opened in 2009—large, art deco–style mobiles hung from high ceilings, wood slatted benches and sturdy tables were placed throughout the space, and brightly colored tables and chairs dotted the children's section—but time and wear had warped everything. The gray carpets were covered in stains from drinks and food and—I'd find out much later—blood.

The children's area was partially separated from the common area by four two-foot-tall bookshelves, and you could see it clearly from most angles in the library. The floor-to-ceiling windows I'd admired could not be opened. There was no source of fresh air, and everything smelled, and felt, stagnant. It reminded me of being on an airplane when a fellow passenger eats fast food, the smell lingering with no way to escape. Whatever scent came into the library stayed. I thought of the concept of "sick building syndrome"—a term used to describe various nonspecific symptoms that occupants of a building experience that cause an increase in sickness and absenteeism. Northwest One seemed like the type of building that might lead to that, if it wasn't already.

From most angles of the library, I could see life outside on busy New Jersey Avenue: cars commuting and people standing at the bus stop or walking quickly to get elsewhere. The people outside commuting—people who, for the most part, did not come into this library—could imagine a calm and quiet library inside.

Until that morning, I had imagined the same.

The children's librarian I was hired to replace had been transferred to a newly renovated library in one of the wealthiest areas of DC. Everyone on staff said that she'd more than earned it after her tenure at Northwest One. I was also told I was much younger and, they hoped, "less old school" and "better at discipline."

When the attached school let out every afternoon, students would arrive to use the computers and socialize at the three tables in the children's section, and groups of teens sometimes came from a nearby middle school and high school. It dawned on me that this might have been why I had been assigned to Northwest One—it was the only library in the system attached to a DC public school. They wanted my school librarian experience.

Before we opened for the day, Frank handed me a lanyard with three keys and a piece of plastic on it. The plastic confused me—I had never seen anything like it.

"And what's this one for?" I asked, fitting my pinkie between the two plastic lines it created and thinking *tuning fork*. It reminded me of my high school band conductor pulling out a metal one, tapping it with a thin metal rod to get our attention.

"Ah, that's to reset the panic button."

I raised my eyebrows. Frank explained that he and Darrion, the adult services librarian, were the only other people in the branch who could reset the button once it was activated. The other staff—Chris, Ms. Williams, Jackie, and Ms. Olson—were not certified librarians, so they did not have one. Frank showed me two discreetly hidden buttons under the circulation desk and explained that when pressed, they would alert both Library Police and the Metropolitan Police Department to an emergency significant enough that staff couldn't safely, or quickly, get to the phone to call 911.

I thought back to a call I'd heard over a walkie-talkie the day before. As part of my DCPL onboarding process, I had been sent to an ominous concrete building in Northeast DC to create my identification and security badge. A voice behind the buzzer at the main door explained I needed to enter when the door unlatched, take the elevator to the third floor, and look for a sign that said LIBRARY POLICE. I assumed the voice was joking—some strange jab at librarians that I was more than used to by then. But when I got off the elevator, I saw the sign hanging in thick red letters above a door: LIBRARY POLICE. (Later that evening I sent a photo of it to friends with a text that read, "Day one. What the fuck?") Inside, an armed officer directed me into a small room where another armed officer sat in front of dozens of television screens. Without looking up, he instructed me to sit in the orange chair and look at the camera. I asked if it was okay to smile, and he slowly turned his body towards me.

"That's up to you."

The flash went off before the words finished coming out of his mouth. We sat in silence for the next few minutes as he punched the information

I'd handwritten on a form into a computer system. I realized that the countless screens in front of him had views from surveillance cameras at each of the library branches. In our silence, I sorted out that each of the 26 branches had four different camera angles on a grid that took up one screen each. Every few minutes, they'd switch to another set of four views.

"What branch are you assigned to?" the officer gruffly asked me.

"Northwest One."

There was a pause.

"And you'll have full security access?"

"I think so?"

He printed my card and handed it to me with something resembling a preamble to a smile. I looked down at the card to see my unsmiling face.

"Well," he said, drawing out the word, "best of luck to you."

I wanted to ask what he meant—why his tone implied I needed a different job more than I needed luck—but he had made it clear we were done speaking.

The whole day had felt this formal. At eight that morning, I'd met with the Human Resources Department on the tenth floor of a different building and had been asked to raise my right hand and recite a legally binding oath to the DC government. My license and passport were taken into another room and scanned. I spent an hour there, mostly filling out paperwork with five other new hires.

When I got up to leave the Library Police headquarters, the officer's walkie-talkie buzzed to life. A voice on the other end said that Captain needed to get over to the Shaw branch to meet two other officers immediately. As I was shutting the door, I heard one more buzz over the radio followed by, "You got that? Immediately!"

I wondered then, and was wondering again now, what emergencies would require the panic button. Frank was visibly eager to move past the topic, and I didn't press him. I knew there would be more time in the coming days to ask, and when we walked into the back office, my concern immediately shifted to where I would sit in the clutter of stacked boxes, office supplies, and cheap desk chairs. The space couldn't have been more than three hundred square feet, and I noticed that behind one of the staff computers a sign read IT HAS BEEN 4 DAYS SINCE OUR LAST INCIDENT. The number four was on a small square of paper, pushed in with a thumbtack. Chris and Darrion told me four days was a pretty good run for Northwest One. The last incident had involved a patron overdosing at a table in the Adult Fiction area. When the paramedics got to the library, they calmly explained that the man was a minute or two away from dying and it had taken two rounds of Narcan to resuscitate him.

"Does that happen a lot here?" I asked.

"It can," Darrion replied. "Don't go back into Adult Fiction alone. Just use the cameras or have one of us go back there." The other two men nodded their agreement.

A minute before our 9:30 opening, a coworker asked if I'd like to come see "the parade." Confused again, I followed them out and stood behind the circulation desk as they unlocked and slammed open the broken doors, pressing the large blue button for the handicap door to let people easily file in. The line—the *parade*, I realized—included more than a dozen people I hadn't seen outside half an hour earlier. The patrons at the front of the line hurried to ask for the only two remaining pairs of working headphones.

Staff called many of the patrons by name as they entered, and Chris shared facts about them to me under his breath. "That's Ms. Greaves. She's been sleeping on the streets for seventeen years, but she used to be an actress." He was pointing out the older woman I'd seen hissing and growling while I waited outside. "And that's Wayne. He's been in recovery for years now, but he comes to the library every day to maintain a sober routine."

Wayne made a point of saying hello to me. He was a ruddy-faced man in his fifties, dressed in clothing that looked noticeably clean and unwrinkled. He'd gotten the first pair of available headphones that morning, handing us his license as collateral. "You're new here!" he'd said, the right side of his mouth lifting into a half smile not unlike the one the library police officer had given me the day before. I introduced myself. He winked and said, "See you around, kid!" He reminded me vaguely of certain of my uncles back home in Buffalo—warm and friendly, but wouldn't take shit or back down from anyone.

Chris quietly told me Wayne had been leaving negative online reviews of the library and library staff for years. I made a mental note: *Wayne, writes Yelp reviews.* I'd always done this with new people—tried to immediately ascribe something about the person to the name so I could remember it: *Ms. Greaves, actress. Young veteran, doesn't give his name, sits in the Fiction A section. Mr. B, very tall and carries a green duffel bag.* It's one of the only surefire ways I can remember multiple new names at once.

After everyone had filed in, Frank asked me to come back into the workroom to complete more onboarding documents. When I sat down next to him, I realized I'd been clenching my jaw. This happened during busy days at the schools sometimes, and I knew to directly address the area, to *tell* it to relax. I felt my back teeth release down in relief just as Darrion came back.

"Frank, we found another one."

Frank's face flushed as he looked from Darrion to me and back to Darrion.

"Where this time?"

"Inside a DVD some guy just returned. I opened it up, and it came crawling out."

Frank was already pulling a trash bag out from his drawer, and he handed it to Darrion before reaching for the phone. He explained that Darrion had found a bedbug and now he was calling to report it to administrators at the downtown office building. Darrion flicked his head back, raised his voice several octaves higher, and said, "This is lunacy!" before heading back out onto the floor. There were still two and a half more hours in his desk shift. There was a brief silence during which Frank and I could both hear the phone pressed to his ear ringing repeatedly. I filled the space by telling Frank I had recently donated games and puzzles from my school library to another school library after they'd had to throw everything out because of a bedbug infestation. He looked relieved.

"They said you'd be a good fit here."

––––––––––

My official title at Northwest One was the grammatically suspect "children librarian." Because the branch was so small and had only one circulation desk, all library workers interacted with all ages. Most other branches in DCPL had large designated children's areas (in some cases, entire floors) that children's librarians manned alone or with other children's librarians. The only specific responsibilities the title gave me at Northwest One were story time leader, liaison to neighborhood schools, and attendee of children's librarians meetings. We hosted two story times each week, and an administrator from the downtown offices was coming to the branch at 9:45 to show me how to lead one. Frank told me Tess had worked as a children's librarian at several branches before accepting an administrative role. She came into the back office a few minutes after Darrion exited.

"We're so excited to have you here with all your school experience," she said warmly. "I know you know how to do a story time, but the idea in DCPL is that if you go to any story time across the District, it should be basically the same. It makes it easier for caregivers and children to participate no matter which branch they're at." Tess showed me a box of items that the former children's librarian had left behind, including a stuffed chicken puppet. When she pulled it out from a drawer, she said, "Perfect! You're gonna need one of these."

Tess, the chicken, and I headed out to the children's area. Already, the branch was busier than fifteen minutes earlier, but the children's area remained empty. Tess optimistically noted that it would be nice to learn with a "small crowd." The former children's librarian had kept two small, colorful carpets wrapped in plastic, to be taken out and used only for story time. They were shoved in a corner of the library, and all I could think about was the bedbug from earlier, and how Darrion had used the words "another one."

A nine-month-old baby named Thomas arrived with his young caregiver and lunged for Chicken, and a minute before 10:00 AM, a young mom and her eight-month-old daughter, Zoe, settled in on the carpet too. Tess was engaging and sweet, and I felt comfort in being around kids again. This was a part of the job that felt the most normal to me, something I could comfortably do.

After story time, I was stuffing Chicken into a filing drawer in the back office when I heard a man screaming and a blue light on the ceiling directly above me started blinking with the same frequency of a strobe.

Tess looked up. "Shit! The panic button." I instinctively touched the plastic shape hanging around my neck.

Out on the floor, ten feet in front of the circulation desk, a bullish man was bent forward, and he was yelling. Books, magazines, and newspapers were strewn all over the floor and desk, and as Tess and I approached the scene he picked up a plastic book club sign and hurled it at Chris. I noticed the story time carpets were empty now, but the front wheels of a stroller were sticking out from behind a bookcase, partially hidden. My heart lurched at the thought of children hiding there.

The man noticed me. "I'll kill you," he yelled. Jabbing a pointer finger at each of us now, standing there in a unified line, he repeated the same threat.

"We understand, sir. We need you to calm down," Frank tried.

"Shut up, you fucking cracker. I'll kill you!"

Everyone on staff stopped speaking as the man continued to yell, but other library patrons were beginning to leave their seats now.

"Man, shut up! You're going to ruin it for everyone!"

He stood his ground for another minute but ran out of nearby things to throw. One last "I'll kill you!" hurled over his shoulder, and he slowly exited the building. Neither of the police departments had arrived yet, despite someone's having pressed the panic button, which I now knew also set off a blue strobe light in the back office.

A few patrons started to silently clean things up. The plastic sign went back on top of a stack of books, two copies of the day's newspaper were neatly refolded and set on the circulation desk, and books on the ground were placed on the reshelving cart. Chris and Frank were pulling surveillance footage for when the police finally arrived, and Darrion shook his head and uttered the refrain that was starting to sound familiar: "Welcome to Northwest One!"

A middle-aged female patron who I'd been told didn't speak to staff unless she absolutely had to approached the desk. "Are those poor children still here?" she quietly asked. I'd seen her grimly watching story time from a nearby table. I thought she'd been annoyed by the singing.

"I'm going to go check on them," I told her.

Thomas's caregiver and Zoe's mom had hidden the children from view as best they could. Zoe's mom peeked her head out as I started walking back and mouthed, "Is he gone?" Zoe was flipping through a board book in her stroller, and Thomas was happily eating a snack from a plastic baggie. The two children and Thomas's caregiver were as unfazed as my coworkers seemed to be. It was only Zoe's mom, new to the neighborhood and library, too, who looked as frazzled as I felt.

"Is this normal?"

"I actually don't know. It's my first day."

She stared back, mouth slightly open, and slowly blinked. "Oh . . ."

On our lunch break I asked Chris what had happened to upset the man so much.

"Frank and I were talking about student loans, and somehow he thought we were talking about him," he explained. "It seemed like he was hallucinating. Maybe thought he was somewhere else and was being threatened? I'm not sure. He's not a regular, so it's harder to know what makes him upset or if he's close to being out of meds. It's early in the month, so it shouldn't be meds. I really don't know. He might be schizophrenic. He was definitely homeless because he asked someone last week about shelter locations."

"We try not to diagnose our customers or talk about their mental health," Frank interjected. "It's not our place to say. We don't know."

"He's probably schizophrenic, though, Frank, don't you think?"

Chris was not just a morning person; he was an all-day person, I realized.

Officially named John Doe0031NW1 in the police report, the man had broken the second rule of category four of the DC Public Library Rules of Behavior: "Directing a specific threat of physical harm against an individual, group of individuals, or property." Chris pointed out the rule in a blue pamphlet that contained all the established rules for the library system. I skimmed the pages, noticing that there were categories of offenses based on severity and age. I saw that any patron who violated a category four rule would be "immediately removed and restricted from all DCPL premises." Since the offender was over eighteen, he would be barred for one to five years, "based on severity."

My mind raced. *Was there a better way to handle the situation and help ease the man out of whatever had upset him so much? Did anyone on staff have a background in social work or de-escalation? What would happen if—when?—someone, maybe even John Doe0031NW1, came in with an actual weapon? Was this a typical response time for emergencies?*

Circling something with questions is how I normally cope with a complex situation—how I imagine many librarians do—but I didn't like any of the answers I came up with. Like employees of the DMV, or restaurants, or hotels, librarians expect to encounter people from many backgrounds, experiences, and moods. Empathy is an essential part of the work if you want to do it in any meaningful way. Find empathy before anger, fear, or confusion. Find empathy before you lose your cool. Find empathy before you lose your shit. Empathy is a first line of defense in public servant jobs—people are less likely to yell at a calm and patient person. Responding with understanding statements like, "It sounds like you've had a really hard day" or "I can understand why you're so upset" can easily de-escalate situations. It can also become incredibly grating to constantly meet unkindness with a version of kindness, gritting your teeth until *nice* comes out. It was particularly hard for me as a woman who sometimes felt, and feels, like our expected neutral state is *nice*.

In the schools, I was larger than most of my students and knew that if I absolutely needed to, I could overpower them. But John Doe had been a grown man who was significantly larger than almost everyone on staff. I didn't know if he would leap across the desk to start attacking me or my coworkers, but his words and demeanor implied he would. It had not been my call to press the panic button and alert the two police groups, but I understood the decision. It had been activated with everyone's physical safety in mind, and in some ways, I felt deeply thankful for it, for the idea that at the press of someone's finger, help would be on the way.

The larger problem I could see was we didn't know what kind of help would show up. Help that would protect us and harm someone else? Help that would demean the severity of what we, or they, were experiencing?

My understanding of the depths of this were minimal at best, but I had not trusted police in well over a decade. From ages nineteen to twenty I had worked at a busy steak house in Buffalo. On several nights when I walked home after midnight, already anxious about being alone so late, Buffalo police officers leaned against their patrol cars and aimed laser pointers at my breasts from the combination gas station and Tim Hortons across the street. I could hear their laughter as they did it, the only sound other than infrequent passing cars that late. The Buffalo Police Department also supposedly hosted private parties above the restaurant, and a female coworker who had worked for the place long enough to bartend for them had explained that they "rounded up" sex workers for the events, giving them the option of being arrested or working for them for the night. None of my experiences with police officers as an adult had been positive, and I did not inherently trust them to protect me.

Next to empathy and pressing the panic button, our collective silence toward John Doe was our best protection as we waited for officers to respond. Frank had tested the waters by replying to him, and we had all seen the response it rendered—more yelling, more throwing of items. Had we kept engaging with him, it likely would have gotten worse. Police from both departments arrived several minutes after John Doe was gone. The end portion of the police report read:

> Subject briefly attempted to go behind the service desk but was blocked from doing so by NW1 staff. Subject then left the building, heading east on L Street. NW1 staff briefly locked the front doors to the building until it was determined that Subject was away from the property and not attempting to reenter. MPD responded and looked over camera footage. Sgt. Victor arrived on scene soon after, followed by Officer Gill and Jones.* Subject John Doe0031NW1 is barred for a total of 5 years for violations of Category 4, Rule #2 (Directing a specific threat of physical harm) and Category 3, Rule #1 (Disruption/disturbance). Subject is unaware of his bar as of 01/10/2018.

I tried to imagine where he would go now that he had a five-year ban from the library. It was the middle of winter, and Chris had confirmed he was experiencing houselessness. There was Dupont Circle and McPherson Square, where groups and individuals often hung out during the day

---

* Officers names have been changed

and slept at night, but neither of them provided any shelter or warmth. Starbucks had not yet changed its policies on loitering, and tent cities were teeming with unsafe conditions. The area shelters were often full, and even though DC had—and has—laws in effect to ensure people are sheltered in below-freezing temperatures, some people, especially those struggling with their mental health, did not feel comfortable going to these locations.

The library was warm. It had fresh water, bathrooms, Internet, newspapers, and the opportunity to socialize. There were no better places I could think of for John Doe0031NW1 to be.

If he couldn't be here, where would he go?

His yelling haunted me for weeks, but this question haunted me for years.

I spent most of the rest of that first shift thinking about what I would do the next time—and it was clear there would be a next time—someone had a violent outburst, but I came to no solid conclusions. I left the branch that day to a chorus of "It was nice to meet you! Maybe we'll see you tomorrow!" and then drove home in rush hour traffic, the Capitol at my back. I thought about whether anyone in any of the offices there had been to Northwest One or any of the DC Public Library branches. I thought about my friends who worked at Smithsonian museums, nonprofits, and law offices around the city. How their day-to-day rarely, if ever, included interactions with people experiencing mental health crises or extreme poverty and houselessness.

And I thought about DC, a city I loved for so many reasons, but had also seen fail its most vulnerable populations, over and over. Systemic injustices ran deep, deep into the bones and marrow of the city, and I recognized how unaware many of the people I knew were of this. To them, DC was where policies and laws were made and changed for the *country*. People lobbied and fought for meaningful change for other states and worked to change overarching laws, but it seemed like many forgot the diverse communities that existed in the diamond shape of the city they lived in. People still often think of DC as a city for politicians and

Hill workers only, but it is a city full of culturally diverse and thriving neighborhoods and communities.

Many of those neighborhoods and communities had, and are, deep into a gentrification that has ripped into rich culture and history all over the country, taking cities from being spaces that provide for poor and middle-class people and "rebuilding" them in the name of capital for the rich. As Peter Moskowitz has written, "Someone who learned about gentrification solely through newspaper articles might come away believing that gentrification is just the culmination of several hundred thousand people's individual wills to open coffee shops and cute boutiques, grow mustaches and buy records. But those are the signs of gentrification, not its causes."[3] The causes, Moskowitz argues, are as old as the United States itself. Gentrification is not possible without something to gentrify, and geographies first have to be made unequal. Similarly, author Jeff Chang writes, "Gentrification is key to understanding what happened to our cities at the turn of the millennium. But it is only half of the story. It is only the visible side of the larger problem: resegregation."[4]

In every afflicted city, the story looks similar. Northwest One, and the Walker-Jones campus attached to it, were surrounded by a neighborhood many people would say was coming back to life. But there had been life there already. It was just being cornered, and erased by, and for, wealth now. Petworth, the neighborhood I lived in, could be described in similar ways.

When I still lived in the Pacific Northwest I went to see the house that inspired the Pixar movie *Up*. The empty and boarded home of Edith Macefield was in Seattle's trendy Ballard neighborhood, awkwardly wedged between an LA Fitness and a UPS store with a wire fence running along the front of it. Tied to the fence was a plastic bag with balloons and markers so visitors could blow up a balloon, write a message on it, and tie it to the fence. When I visited in 2015, most of the balloons tied to the fence were deflated, creating a weeping splash of color to the front of an already sad-looking house, in an area full of gray buildings.

I searched the wrinkled writing on the balloons. There were wishes for ailing family members to heal, birth and death dates, names and dates to prove a couple had been there. The balloons were not for Edith or Seattle or the neighborhood that had built up around the home. They were, it seemed, mostly for tourists. I couldn't bring myself to write on a balloon. I had people I loved and was missing, people I wanted to name and remember as many ways as I could, but not on these balloons outside a home someone had fought so hard to keep in a city that wanted it demolished for its own profit. It was the saddest place I could think of for remembering a loved one or making a wish.

As the story goes, Edith Macefield refused a $1 million offer to sell her house to commercial developers in the Ballard neighborhood in 2006, forcing the planned five-story commercial building project to go up around her 108-year-old farmhouse. She died in the house in 2008 at age eighty-six as construction continued around her. A year after her death, Disney publicists attached balloons to the roof of the house as a promotional tie-in for *Up*, which grossed $735.1 million worldwide. In 2013, the inaugural Macefield Music Festival was in Ballard with the promoters saying the event would be "an affordable way to explore the current landscape of Seattle music while celebrating the steadfast attitude of the dearly departed Ms. Macefield."[5] Her cause, again, sold for profit. Her memory tokenized for tourists and passersby.

Northwest One reminded me of Edith's house. It was awkwardly sandwiched and forgotten by most people who passed by, but sometimes nostalgia pulled locals in. They'd walk by, realize it was a public library, and come through its doors to tell us how glad they were to discover it. Most of these types of visitors took one lap around the small branch, browsed a few shelves, and slowly began to really take in the space, and the other patrons. Occasionally they'd sign up for a library card, but more often, they'd smile a sadder smile than the one they came in with as they passed me at the circulation desk to leave the branch without ever coming back.

One middle-aged woman who visited in this way approached the desk at the end and asked in a whisper, "Why are there no children here? This is devastating." Her face looked pained, and it took everything for me to not respond, "What are you going to do about it?"

Every time something like this happened, I thought about Edith's home. Maybe for a moment while visitors, or even locals, stood in front of the house, they thought about the history of the city and what, and who, had been expelled from comfortably living in it. Maybe, when people stopped into Northwest One randomly, they had these pauses as well. Maybe they thought about it for hours, days, months afterward. I couldn't know. What I did know was that I rarely saw any of them come back to the branch.

———

A few days after my first shift, I remembered to read Wayne's Yelp reviews. His most recent was dated December 2017, less than a month before I started:

> The Library from "L" not liking people with disabilities the Librarians will make rude comments to one another like kids at a broadcast booth. #1 Homeless stop, Library has had armed Cop(s) sit in children's section plus Rats feast outside.

I understood Wayne's desire to write his reviews. Over the nine months I worked at Northwest One, I saw many of our patrons writing by hand on scrap paper, and with time and developed trust, I got to read some of the pages. Sometimes they contained obsessive and intrusive thoughts, but more often it was notes about their daily lives. One regular patron asked me for a single piece of notebook paper every day. She'd settle in at a table with a golf pencil to write, and after a week, she asked if she could show me what she had been working on. A stack of paper, crinkled and smudged with pencil lead, was in front of her.

"It's my memoir," she explained.

On the top of the first page she'd written the title in all capital letters: *MY ANIMAL LIFE.*

"It's about my life out here, you know?"

I encouraged her to keep going and then asked Frank if I could take my lunch break early. I walked three blocks, sat down on a bench underneath a luxury apartment building, and cried. The woman had wanted to be seen and writing was one way. I think this was the main motivation behind Wayne's reviews, too, despite his genuine and prevailing disdain toward most of the staff. Any time someone Googles

"Northwest One," Wayne will be there. I understand this stake he's made, and he deserves it.

In my own private notebook, I had written this about my first day:

> Watching patrons enter the library this morning, with their suitcases and bags and layers, watching my coworkers call them by their names, or by sir or madam, with dignity, with appreciation and respect, has been one of the most beautiful experiences of my life. They have a routine here. They have quiet and a safe space. When our coworkers banded behind the circulation desk today, our patrons gathered around the other side of it, ready to protect us. Ready to protect their space. It is an honor and a privilege to be in service to the people this city seems to have forgotten.

I still more or less understand these words, but I also see a layer of the kind of thinking so typical of White people especially. *I help others, isn't that great. We all need to be kinder to each other!* Kindness in particular is often something that's preached when we know any significant and powerful change will also require grit, anger, disturbance, discomfort, and pushing against the status quo, sometimes with our bodies. Kindness is an entry and starting point for change, and it is crucial. But to fully enact and embody the work we need to see in public libraries, kindness is not nearly enough on its own.

PART II

EMPATHY

5

CAN YOU HELP ME?

If it is inaccessible to the poor, it is neither radical nor revolutionary.

—Jonathan Herrera

THE DC PUBLIC LIBRARY was founded in 1896 by an Act of Congress, set up as an independent agency of the District of Columbia. It was intended to serve as the "people's university" and would "furnish books and other printed matter and information service convenient to the homes and offices of all residents of the District."[1] Theodore W. Noyes, the editor of the *Evening Star*, a DC newspaper that circulated between 1852 and 1981, campaigned for years for the establishment of a tax-sustained free public library in DC and was largely responsible for its founding. Noyes served for fifty years on the Board of Library Trustees that Congress also established to set policy for the library to ensure it maintained its independence in the District, a board that remains today.

From 1898 to 1903, the first DC public library was in a house at 1326 New York Avenue NW. Funds donated by Andrew Carnegie in 1899 allowed for them to build and open a central library in Mount Vernon Square, with President Theodore Roosevelt in attendance at the dedication ceremony in 1903. In total, Carnegie funded three branch libraries in DC, with the first opening in the Takoma neighborhood in 1911. The Mount Vernon Square library was subsequently renamed Central Public Library and moved to a larger location in 1972, where it still remains today as the central branch of DCPL: the Martin Luther King Jr. Memorial Library.[2]

As of 2021, the DC Public Library system includes twenty-five neighborhood libraries in addition to the central branch. The current Board of Library Trustees is made up of nine unpaid District residents from wards around the city. Board members are appointed by the mayor and confirmed by the DC Council for a maximum of two five-year terms, with the District's chief financial officer providing a fiscal officer to ensure that financial practices within DCPL meet the District requirements. It is the role of the chief librarian/executive director to oversee and manage a team of nearly thirty administrators and the role of the library chief of staff to oversee a team of four additional administrators. These staff have a variety of responsibilities including operations, fiscal management, and carrying out policies made by the board, and include roles like a director of customer experience, director of contracts and procurement, director of service design and engagement, and two codirectors of neighborhood libraries.[3]

During my employment, deciphering who made what decisions within DCPL was not something I easily understood, even with access to an organizational chart that outlined who answered to whom. While we had regular communications from the executive director and other administrative folks through e-mail and at regularly scheduled meetings, I mostly answered to Frank, my coworkers, and the patrons in the day-to-day, and I preferred it this way.

When I showed up to Northwest One each day, it felt possible to do good. It felt like an important place to be—not important like there was any sort of power I wanted to yield or bestow, but important like I was a contributing member of an institution that, by its nature, was resolute in caring for members of the DC community, not just the politicians and Hill workers and transplants for summer internships. The library was open to all, but it also regularly served the people who work, grieve, eat, fight, sleep, and truly *live* in DC.

Every day, patrons needed something, and as they searched and received or found and learned, I did too. Not all the work at the branch was draining or defeating. Much of it was social and engaging, and I certainly was never bored at work. I enjoyed when someone saw a headline in the day's newspaper and wanted to tear into it for a few minutes with me. I looked forward to phone calls from elderly patrons who needed help using Google. I liked processing the books people put on hold and discovering which names checked out stacks of books I began to build my own reading lists around. I enjoyed getting to know many of the regular patrons who were, for better and worse, people I spent nearly forty hours a week with.

I began to know and care for my coworkers, too. Darrion's dry sense of humor and contrarian nature made for animated conversations in the back office, ones where I felt safe asking questions or sharing still-processing thoughts, which came as a relief in an environment that was often nearly impossible to process in real time. I realized at Northwest One that I externally process only with people I feel safe with, and with Chris and Darrion, especially, I did. My job at Northwest One was the first time I had ever felt completely free and accepted in my profession to be myself. In school staff meetings I was almost always silent, even when I had something to contribute. I knew it was not the environment to offer up something like, "Have we considered how making students take a test to determine which of Howard Gardner's multiple intelligences they fall under might also be teaching students one more way to categorize themselves rather than explore their natural interests and evolve more holistically into who they are?" or "Do you know the etymology of the word *quiz*? It's fascinating!"

My questions required energy and time, and K–12 educators can attest to the fact that there is very little of both in a school day. But at the public library, at Northwest One, Chris and Darrion always went with my outbursts, questions, and concerns in similar ways. We would sit quietly in the back room at our individual computers until someone offered up something—sometimes it had to do with the work, sometimes it was just our random curiosities—and we'd each give our thoughts, search for additional information, and above all else, listen and process, together.

We treated each other like intelligent and capable individuals who were curious and well intentioned, but also human and fallible. We naturally bounced ideas and thoughts off one another, genuinely seeking each other's thinking, including criticism and pushback. It was this that was essential to our bond: any disagreement came with an unspoken agreement that it did not lessen our views of one another as humans. In hindsight, I was learning to think more critically, and I had a safe environment in which to do so. Darrion and Chris quickly became, and remain, two of my favorite and most trusted people.

Out on the library floor, Darrion was steady and calm under even the most dramatic stressors. He would sit stoically as a patron yelled at him, waiting until the worst of it was done before responding in an even tone. He was often the person to talk me down after a bad incident. Chris was similarly calm, but much more extroverted than Darrion. He regularly engaged with patrons, helping them work on résumés and job applications and holding long conversations with them at the circulation desk.

Both men supported my autonomy in the work and only intervened in interactions with patrons if I asked them to. I knew they would defend me if I needed it, but perhaps more importantly, I knew that they respected and trusted my abilities. In the early days at Northwest One I looked forward to work because I knew they were there. In the later days, I knew I could make it through any day if one of them was there also. Darrion and Chris were both hoping to leave Northwest One, though. Chris had been hired a year before me as a library associate but had his degree in international studies and was in the middle of a lengthy hiring process for a high-clearance government job. Darrion was hoping for a branch change, as he had been at Northwest One for more than three years and that was generally about how long it took for people to be reassigned.

Chris and Darrion were aware, and vocal, about the many issues at the branch. We were bonded almost immediately, and then only more deeply, by the experiences of the day-to-day work. There was nothing I could not say to either of them, and there was nothing they could not say to me about the daily atmosphere and work. We all understood the exhaustion, anger, trauma, and sadness of it all and that these feelings sometimes came in overwhelming waves that compromised our abilities to be professional or to uphold our better sides. More times than I can remember, I said something in the back office that ultimately I did not mean. Chris and Darrion knew this inherently. I was deeply thankful for the mutual respect, humility, and care that existed between us.

Frank, like any manager or boss, had to walk a fine line between overseeing our work and being our friend. He sometimes joined in the animated back-office conversations with Darrion and Chris and revealed his own thoughts about the struggles at Northwest One. He was also pragmatic—a former solider who had served multiple tours in Iraq and had a certain level of soldierlike control and order that permeated all his actions and conversations. He explained to me once that he always tried to assume the best about people's intentions first, never the worst, and I saw him maintain this attitude with coworkers, patrons, and administrators. I usually felt comfortable speaking to him about concerns, but as I'd seen with the incident with Christian, I would not always like his responses.

Our small staff included two library technicians and two additional library associates. Our children's library associate was a woman in her forties named Jackie. For the most part, Jackie did not seem to enjoy her work at the library, and she was often vocal about this as well as rude and dismissive to patrons. If she was listening to a podcast she particularly liked or deep into watching videos on YouTube, she'd remove one earbud and say, "Nope!" or "Not now!" to patrons who approached the desk. She could be responsive and kind, especially with children, but often it seemed like that happened only when she felt like it. The work at the library had worn her down, too. I had unknowingly disrespected her early on by giving her only a few days' notice that I would be away from the branch at a training on the day we typically held story time. Our communication styles differed and what I had thought was direct communication had been interpreted as flippant and uncaring. From then on, when I was on the desk with her, she often told patrons, "Not me, her," and would tilt her head or point a finger my way, even if I was already helping someone, or helping someone with two or three people already in line behind them. I was never able to "win" Jackie over, and eventually, in my own state of burnout, I stopped wanting to. She sometimes called patrons and coworkers "retarded," "crazy," "stupid" to their faces and more than once had escalated situations unnecessarily, especially with patrons struggling with their mental health. In the greater scheme of the daily stress and chaos of Northwest One, addressing Jackie's actions fell to the bottom of the priority list for everyone. We needed each staff member to man the branch, and no one in the system wanted to be reassigned to Northwest One. Our second library associate joined the branch part-time three months into my work there. Kenleigh was a former Baltimore public school teacher and was finishing her MLS degree. She was a few years younger than me and also White. She ran a Bookstagram where she posted reviews of books alongside photos of baked goods from around the DC area. She quickly and easily became friendly with Chris, Darrion, and me and joined us in lively back-office conversations.

The two library technicians, Ms. Williams and Ms. Olson, had both worked for the DC Public Library for more than twenty years and had been at Northwest One since the branch first opened in 2009. Ms. Williams had sole custody of her grandson, Damon, and fostered children as well. Every so often, she'd come to work with a new little boy or girl and Damon in tow. Damon went to the public school attached to the library and was a bright spot in each of our days.

Ms. Olson was funny, deeply faithful, and had a no-nonsense attitude. Oftentimes anything she mumbled under her breath made me laugh so hard she'd turn and say, "You heard that?" and laugh along with me. She'd returned to the branch a few weeks after I started after recovering from a heart attack. She was deeply set in her ways and had designated spots in the back office and at the circulation desk that she'd decorated with personal photos and printed pages of Bible scripture. I had once borrowed a pen from her computer desk cup and gotten an earful the next day when she discovered I had put it back in a different cup at a different computer.

All the staff members went by their first names, except for Ms. Williams and Ms. Olson, and I was told on day one to never call either of them by theirs. It was a matter of respect—they were the matriarchs of large families and knew the branch, the patrons, and the neighborhood better than anyone else. They had little patience for complaining and certainly not for dramatics. Once, when I had left several Fiction books on the return cart to avoid entering the Adult Fiction area, Ms. Williams asked me, "Who's going to do that for you?" Ms. Olson had laughed, nodded, and said, "Not me, baby. Not me."

The two women were deeply kind and supportive. One morning on my way into work I had stopped at a red light a mile away from the branch, and a man who had been aggressively tailgating me got out of his car and approached the window. I had foolishly rolled it down to engage, and he reached in to grab me and then my phone, which he then threw down onto the pavement. Before the light turned green, I had collected my phone, taken a photo of his license plate, said "Fuck you!" and gotten back into my car to finish the drive to work. It was the autopilot I had learned at the branch—respond, protect, move on. But I was shaken up and almost immediately started to cry when I explained to Ms. Williams, Ms. Olson, and our custodian, Ms. Nadine, what had happened. They encouraged me to call the police to file a report and took over my morning responsibilities so I could have time to collect myself in the back office while I waited for an officer to respond.

They reminded me in many ways of my own mother, who had never coddled me during my late teens and early twenties as I started to navigate the world more independently. My second week on the job, Ms. Williams had told me, "We're a family here." I smiled and nodded, but wrote her words off. Any time a coworker or boss had called work a family in my past, it had felt like a way to coerce us into additional labor or to ignore some glaring imbalance of power or responsibilities. But Ms. Williams meant family like the people who look out for you, no matter what. She meant family like *I will put myself on the line for you*. This kind of family I understood; it was the kind I had grown up with in Buffalo.

There was no one on staff who I did not trust to put their body on the line for another, if necessary. All of us—Frank, Darrion, Chris, Ms. Williams, Ms. Olson, Jackie, and Kenleigh—worked together as a team as well as we could in the cramped, shared space that was Northwest One. We were all strong at different tasks, and with different patrons, but we banded together whenever it was necessary.

One of the main job responsibilities at Northwest One, one that we all shared, was manning the library's only circulation desk. Every morning there was a schedule for the day that included at least one two-to-three-hour shift at the desk. Usually at least two people at a time were assigned to the desk, but there were sometimes more depending on the hour of the day. It was uncommon to only have one person, but it happened sometimes.

There were three chairs and three computers behind the L-shaped wooden circulation desk, and the short side was to patrons' right as soon as they entered the branch. Ms. Williams liked to sit in this first chair, monitoring who came in. The next seat, on the longer part of the desk, was the spot Ms. Olson and Jackie preferred. The chair at the very end of the long side of the desk was what we all referred to as the "hot seat." Frank, Darrion, Chris, Kenleigh, and I all regularly ended up sitting there on desk shifts. There was no barrier to the right of this chair and we regularly had to ask patrons to come around to the front, not sidle up next to us. It was the desk spot that patrons approached the most.

Directly behind the length of the desk was a countertop where we kept books until their release dates along with other items we regularly needed to process books. Underneath this counter were plastic blue bins for books being sent out or received, and this was also where a baseball bat that had the word SLUGGER written on it in large white letters leaned. It was a leftover from a former manager at the branch who was now a library administrator. The bat was meant as a joke whose evolution I now forget, but more than once I had watched an employee slowly move closer to it during violent incidents.

Whenever someone approached the circulation desk at the library, it usually began with one question: "Can you help me?" I have heard this asked with humor, anger, sadness, joy, and defeat. I have heard it whispered and spoken much louder, even shouted. I have heard "Can you help me?" from people of all ages, genders, races, and backgrounds. It is a question that reflects what all of us want: to be seen, heard, and helped when we ask for help.

In 2019 DCPL had 3,820,005 library visitors, and the system's 125 librarians with MLS degrees (and presumably some of the 415 other staff) engaged in 839,892 reference transactions throughout the year.[4] A single reference transaction can range from one question to dozens and can last from a few seconds to much longer. I showed up at the library each day believing I could help, ready for this question, even wanting to hear it. There was a distinct breath I took in these moments, just before a patron spoke. The briefest recognition of the rise and fall of my chest, preparing myself for what might be coming next. Like opening a box of hats and thrusting my arms into it, fingertips on four or five, ready to pull what I needed.

All librarians know this moment, this pause, when you're trying to guess what a person might need help with. The longer I worked at Northwest One, the better I got at guessing those needs before people spoke. *It's been fifteen minutes, Ms. Connor is going to want an express pass for the computer again,* or *Mr. Bard wants to tell me that someone in the computer lab turned off the fan again.* Sometimes, though, questions surprised me. Being a librarian in DC meant regularly being asked for the address of the FBI or where someone might find and talk to a CIA agent or how and where they might begin research about a specific conspiracy theory they believed in. Sometimes patrons just wanted information about how to get a Library of Congress reader's card, or they needed help finding a public shower and a hot meal. Several times I met patrons who had recently been released from prison and needed someone to show them how to sign up for an e-mail address. Many times, I was called into the computer lab to help with basic computer skills, showing patrons how they could delete more than one e-mail at a time or explaining that pop-up ads were common and not a virus.

The list of things people come to a library for help with, or end up wanting help with once they are at the library, is unending. Sometimes I was an information professional, providing a quick answer, printing walking directions, advising which Metro stop was closest. Other times, I was a social worker or mental health advocate, speaking to someone through a psychotic episode or guiding them through the steps necessary to secure a shelter bed that night. Other times I was a first responder. A patron once came in holding his left hand tightly with his right, and he asked for a Band-Aid. As I gathered the first aid kit and the man gingerly opened his palm, I saw that it looked like he had been stabbed. I calmly told him that I didn't think a Band-Aid would be enough and asked if I could call paramedics for him. He responded no and asked for the gauze roll, which I gave to him. As he wrapped his hand, he explained that he could not remember how or when the injury had happened, just that he woke up bleeding a lot. There were many times when people arrived with injuries or ailments that I could, quite literally, only offer a Band-Aid for. Sometimes I was a confidant, mediator, or reporter at the desk, just listening to people's stories. Always, I was a witness, even if I did not want to be.

Most of the regular patrons at Northwest One were unhoused, and many of them were also struggling with addiction, their mental health, or a broad range of symptoms from experienced trauma. Often, they were struggling with a combination of all these things, as the percentages of people experiencing houselessness also have much higher propensities for psychotic illness, personality disorders, major depression, and alcohol and drug dependence.[5] I saw this reflected clearly at Northwest One. And although I started each day with a drive to help, there were things I simply could not fix. Things no librarian can.

This is one of the more crushing aspects of the profession—knowing that you are leaving someone feeling unhelped or even helpless. This inability to address the broader or more systemic problems, and the situations that grew from those roots, eventually led to my own deep feelings of helplessness. I ended every day in my first two months at Northwest One by driving home to my apartment to sit in silence, assessing the day. I lived alone, and although I had friends who would have happily met me for dinner or a drink, I could not fathom being around anyone else after work. I lay on my cheap and uncomfortable couch from Walmart and wondered what more I could have done, or what I could have done differently, that day. I often spent hours online looking for resources and guidance. Nothing ever felt like enough, and the question that always remained unanswered was, *Where else could they go for the help they needed?*

It was a question I often posed to others in my years as a librarian: where else, other than a library, can people facing housing insecurity go for the entire day and not be kicked out? Twice, in DC, a person responded "Museums!" as the seventeen Smithsonian museums are all free and open to the public. But security at the Smithsonian eventually asks unhoused people to leave, too, due to any number of violations of rules around conduct, loitering, volume and language, and drug use. Underserved populations who might otherwise find refuge in America's public city spaces are often met with rules that are meant to create a barrier between them and tourists—a barricade between them and beautiful architecture, design, and other facades that are, we might infer, viewed as more valuable to protect and preserve than human lives.

Despite also catering to tourists and more middle-class individuals, many city neighborhood library branches are by their nature a more accommodating—more understanding and empathetic—place for unhoused persons. A visitor can move more freely and comfortably in the space, with Wi-Fi, clean drinking water, bathroom facilities, conversation, and other basic comforts available without as much judgment or being ejected on grounds of trespassing.

It is what vulnerable populations of people are readily able to access at libraries that I've found makes some people most uncomfortable. Clean bathrooms mean people can bathe, brush their teeth, shave, and take care of other hygiene matters the way most do in the privacy of their own homes. Restroom stalls or single-use bathrooms can make for a preferred place to use drugs. Internet access means an ability to view pornography or adult content, and it also means anyone sitting nearby might see it. A safe and comfortable place for a single parent living out of their car means hearing babies and children cry throughout the day, sometimes for long stretches, in a library many assume should be quiet. Relaxed rules about eating mean everyone is subjected to the smell and sound of the meals. If someone approached the circulation desk with a complaint about any of these things, they almost always said the same thing: this is the *library*. And many times, the people who were complaining were other regular patrons who wanted the library to be a more comfortable space for them and others.

I am not unsympathetic to these frustrations. Of course it is unpleasant to smell severe body odor or step onto a floor wet with someone's bathwater or any of the other possibilities when a space is truly open to all community members. Of course. These people complaining have the right to want a less chaotic setting.

But the reality is this *is* the library.

It is not the library of our ideals—the one where it is always quiet, pristine, stately, where the space is treated with an almost holy reverence for its inherent cultural value and the computer lab is mostly for printing emergencies. This version of the library exists in some locations for certain, but it is becoming more and more a national fantasy, one that we see in our films and books that are set in the center of prestigious universities, usually privately funded, or located in sweeping suburbs or wealthier neighborhoods in our cities. These interpretations of libraries only capture a small percent of them—tied, more often than not, to the socioeconomic status and demographics of the populations they serve.

For the last ten years, whenever I visit a new place, I try to also visit a library there. I have visited rural towns, large cities, and suburbs across the country from Denver to Buffalo to Missoula to Joshua Tree. In those ten years, I have yet to walk into a public library where there is not someone there utilizing the space to meet some sort of basic need that they cannot fulfill as easily elsewhere. What many people still consider the exception—"Ah, that's just in cities!"—is, in actuality, the rule. It is just a difficult one to sit with.

This upheld idea and ideal of public libraries becomes a tool against marginalized groups. When we call libraries "social equalizers" or "safe havens," we don't have to worry so much about what happens to that equality and safety outside the library. I experienced the many dichotomies within the library with similar discomfort, and sometimes disgust, as some visitors. But I also began, mostly out of desperation for answers, to more closely understand the many layers of *why* so many libraries have become a refuge for marginalized groups.

6

COLD MERCY

No moral code or ethical principle, no piece of scripture
or holy teaching, can be summoned to defend what we
have allowed our country to become.

—Matthew Desmond, *Evicted: Poverty and Profit in the
American City*

ANY GOOD INQUIRY STARTS WITH A QUESTION, but I also believe that any
good inquiry ends on a new question or questions. *I've solved this piece,
but in that search, I discovered this, which also needs answering.* It happens
again and again, and I do not find the cycle maddening or inefficient or
frustrating. I find it profoundly freeing and a reminder that everything in
our world is deeply connected. For me, the question that naturally comes
next is: how did houselessness become so rampant in America that many
public libraries have begun to serve as day shelters?

In looking at this refuge in the public library, it is essential to examine
the history of what many journalists and scholars refer to as the current
"homeless crisis" in America. Our modern era of houselessness can be
best traced back to the early 1980s, when several major forces changed its
complexion: gentrification of the inner city, sweeping deinstitutionalization, budget cuts to the US Department of Housing and Urban Development (HUD) and social services agencies in response to the country's
worst recession since the Great Depression, high unemployment rates, the
emergence of HIV/AIDS, and inadequate amounts of affordable housing

options.[1] Additionally, rents in metro areas have been increasing while wages have remained stagnant,[2] as evidenced by the federal minimum wage still being $7.25 as of 2021, having last been raised in 2009.

How the library became an epicenter of this crisis is intimately tied to these many factors, but given that the population I served at Northwest One were overwhelmingly struggling with their mental health, I became particularly interested in the impact of the deinstitutionalization of mental health facilities in the 1960s, '70s, and '80s. Civil rights and civil liberties movements of the 1960s, especially, envisioned more fulfilling lives for patients who had been living in understaffed state psychiatric hospitals, and advocates remained hopeful—and vocal—about new medications and community-based services that could replace the need for so many patients to live in those state hospitals.[3] There was a growing public awareness of the inhumane conditions in many psychiatric hospitals as national magazines like *Life* and *Reader's Digest* published articles and exposés detailing the neglect and abuse that were common at institutions where patients greatly outnumbered hospital staff, many of whom were poorly trained. President John F. Kennedy signed the Community Mental Health Act in 1963 as the first of multiple federal initiatives to create a more community-based system of care. In his message delivered to Congress on February 5, 1963, proposing the legislation, Kennedy emphasized the shift: "When carried out, reliance on the cold mercy of custodial isolation will be supplanted by the open warmth of community concern and capability. Emphasis on prevention, treatment and rehabilitation will be substituted for a desultory interest in confining patients in an institution to wither away."[4]

In 1965, under President Lyndon B. Johnson, Congress passed the Medicaid Act, which offered higher reimbursement rates for community-based care and excluded payments to mental health institutions. A few years later, the Supplemental Security Income (SSI) disability benefits program provided direct financial support for eligible individuals with mental illness living in the community. This rapid shift away from institutionalization was encouraged by federal legislation, policy changes, and litigation that incentivized and eventually mandated public mental health systems to shift the locus of care to the community. The community was not adequately prepared. In the 1975 US Supreme Court case of *O'Connor v. Donaldson*, it was declared that a person had to be a danger to themself or to others for a hospital confinement to be constitutional. As it became increasingly harder for people to be admitted to a hospital, many people with severe mental illness ended up unhoused. By 1980, the inpatient population at public psychiatric hospitals had declined by 75 percent. In 2000, approximately fifty-five thousand people remained in these institutions, a number less than 10 percent of those in institutions fifty years prior. Forward movement rooted in supporting deinstitutionalization continued. In 1996, the DC Court of Appeals case *Lake v. Cameron* introduced the concept of a "least restrictive setting" and required hospitals to discharge patients to an environment less restrictive than a hospital if at all possible. The 1999 US Supreme Court decision in *Olmstead v. L.C.* stated that mental illness was a disability covered under the Americans with Disabilities Act, requiring that all governmental agencies, not just the state hospitals, were required to make "reasonable accommodations" to move people with mental illness into community-based treatment to end unnecessary institutionalization.[5] The shift was especially pronounced among children and youth: by 2009, the institutionalized population had declined by 98 percent.[6]

This is certainly not an exhaustive list of the many initiatives and legal proceedings that changed the scope and ease of access to mental health care. And while these decisions certainly led to important and significant progress in preserving the rights of people struggling from severe mental illness, public mental health systems largely failed to develop sufficient resources and staffing to treat and support people in home and community-based settings, leaving many with inadequate supports to remain safely in their own homes and communities. In 2006, psychiatrist Darold Treffert profoundly described how laws had gone too far in protecting the rights of the individual at the expense of their own safety and well-being as "dying with one's rights on."[7] All of this has led to increased risks, and numbers, of people with mental illness experiencing substance abuse disorders, suicide, and houselessness, with 20.5 percent of unhoused people in the United States having a serious mental health condition.

The current decentralized mental health system has predominantly benefited middle-class people with less severe disorders who are able to reenter their homes and communities more easily. Most people with severe mental health issues still receive inadequate services and have a difficult time integrating into a community, where they become even more vulnerable. People living with untreated mental conditions are sixteen times more likely to be shot and killed by police.[8] And of those who survive outside of help from the system, many end up in prison. Crime, of course, is not arbitrary. Most of the time, it happens when people have been unable to meet their basic needs through other means, and people struggling with their mental health often have a much more difficult time doing so.

Between 2019 and 2021, about two million times per year people with serious mental illness were booked into jails, with an estimated four thousand of them held in solitary confinement inside US prisons. Sixty-six percent of women in prison report having a history of mental illness, which is almost twice the percentage of men in prison. Three in five people with a history of mental illness do not receive mental health treatment while incarcerated in either state or federal prisons. Less than half of people with a history of mental illness receive mental health treatment while held in local jails. Among incarcerated people with a mental health condition, non-White people are more likely to go to solitary confinement, be injured, and stay in jail longer.[9] And it should be common knowledge that the three largest public mental health providers in America are correctional systems: Los Angeles County, Rikers Island in New York, and Cook County in Illinois.[10]

———

There are few better examples of the loss of essential services and supports for unhoused people within DC than the Franklin School Shelter at Thirteenth and K Streets NW. At seven in the morning on September 26, 2008, city representatives woke up the remaining people at the men-only homeless shelter located there and asked them to leave immediately. They briefly explained that workers were coming to pack up beds, furniture, and supplies. Lawyer and advocate Jane Zara, present on scene, observed a police car parked outside with a loudspeaker repeating that the shelter had been closed and also noted that the men in the shelter that day lost their identification as they were removed from the building, compromising their abilities to seek employment or even gain entrance to many government buildings to apply for many benefits and services. Men who arrived at the shelter later in the day, hoping to sleep there that night, were also turned away. Over the next several months, the Committee to Save Franklin Shelter filed two lawsuits against the city, one in DC Superior Court and one in federal court, and they lost both cases.

If you looked up the Franklin School Shelter on Google Maps in 2018 it was a gray rectangle surrounded by similar building shapes that were peach colored, signifying that they were occupied. The otherwise all-occupied buildings nearby looked like they had flesh and were still breathing, and the Franklin School stood out as a lifeless gray mark. Other than a brief occupation by Occupy DC protesters in 2011, the building remained empty after that 2008 morning when residents were kicked out and promised alternative housing that was never secured for them. Many of these people considered the Franklin School Shelter something of a home base or, at a minimum, a safer place to sleep than outside, and many of them opted to stay as close to the familiar building as they could: on a park bench across the street in Franklin Square Park.

I walked through Franklin Square Park, and past the Franklin School Shelter, every morning Monday through Friday for the first three years I lived in DC. Each morning, every bench in the park had a person sleeping on it. When all the benches were taken, people slept on the ground, wrapped in human-sized gray cocoons of wool blankets someone from somewhere passed out.

I will never forget what it felt like to walk around shapes of sleeping people every day, especially in the winter months or in the extreme heat of DC's lengthy summers. Even when the climate cooperated, they were still constantly exposed to theft, assault, rape, sickness, and other inhumane conditions and indignities. During every busy downtown morning commute, people hustled past them, including me. I had hundreds of students I was walking to at Thomson, many of them living far below the poverty line and experiencing houselessness too. Some of my students' families shared one-bedroom apartments with each other, up to ten people sometimes in a single unit. These students sometimes went to unpack lunches with cockroaches inside and told their teachers how they had not slept well the night before because of rats or mice crawling on them. These students were young, and it felt more possible to help them than the grown men and women on the benches. But still, every morning I was reminded of the adults whom the city had forgotten.

In October of 2020, the Franklin School Shelter became the home of a private language arts museum called Planet Word, with the tagline "The museum where language comes to life." The $66 million museum was created by real estate heiress and former teacher named Ann Friedman. The museum pays the city $10 a year on a ninety-nine-year lease for the historic building.

I learned that the museum includes an interactive piece at its entrance called *Speaking Willow*, a motion-detecting tree sculpture that whispers to visitors in hundreds of languages. Other exhibits in the museum have names alluding to language, voice, and communication: *Where Do Words Come From?* and *The Spoken World* and *First Words*. One October 2020 article in the *Washington Post* called a visit to Planet Word a "high-tech, feel-good experience," but all I could think about was who had lived in the space a little over a decade earlier.

Who heard them? Who valued their words? How had they tried to communicate?

The Franklin School Shelter is just one of multiple DC housing accommodations that have abruptly closed and displaced people living in the District with no solid plan to support them. The city has also closed the makeshift homeless shelters at the Motel 6 on Georgia Avenue NW, the Ivy City Hotel on New York Avenue NE, and DC General, a former hospital that housed more than 260 families a night up until May 2018. As of this writing, none of them have been adequately replaced.

In an additional blow to the unhoused population living in the area, Franklin Square Park closed for renovations in July 2020 to make it "more user-friendly."[11] Plans included restoring the tree canopy, eliminating rodent infestations, replacing paths, and installing rain gardens. These changes certainly improved the appeal to many of the people who work in the area, patronize the local businesses, or visit as tourists, but they also effectively exiled the twenty or so unhoused people who had still been living in the park. In some acknowledgment of this impact, a senior adviser to DC mayor Bowser stated that the renovation was "not intended to displace anyone but to beautify downtown Washington," adding that it would make the park a major attraction for the city, with a note that DC is one of the few cities of its size that doesn't have an urban park within it. In the same article, the clinical director for the DC homeless outreach organization Street Sense said Franklin Park's closure would negatively affect a population that "has already borne more than its share of tumult."[12]

Once again, preference was given to the profits of tourism and the comforts of only some.

———————

Every year a regional census of the houseless population in DC, called the Point-in-Time (PIT) count, takes place in a single twenty-four-hour period, typically at night and in the last ten days of January. According to the 2020 results, 6,380 people were experiencing houselessness in the District, though this number accounts only for those who were unsheltered or staying in an emergency shelter or transitional housing, not those couch surfing, in hospitals, jails, treatment facilities, or living in their cars, and so forth. In 2018, when I worked at Northwest One, the number was 6,904.[13]

The reality that houselessness affects people of all races, genders, and ages is something all librarians and city workers can speak to, but data shows that persons who are Black or African American are disproportionately affected by the drivers of houselessness in the District. As of 2020, 5,823 out of 6,380 or 91.3 percent of adults who were experiencing houselessness are Black/African American (In 2018, it was 6,286 persons out of 6,904 or 91 percent),[14] yet only 46 percent of District residents are Black/African American.[15] Washington, DC, also has the highest rate in the country of adults with dependence or abuse of illicit drugs or alcohol at 12.51 percent of its population, with the national average being 8.47 percent. The percent of adults experiencing houselessness and also substance use and mental health concerns was 45.1 percent of single adults and 13.5 percent of adults in families for a total of 38.7 percent of adults. Broken down by gender, 47.6 percent of single women and 44.1 percent of single men reported substance use and mental health conditions. Within the larger DC population, 19.32 percent has a diagnosed mental illness (the national average is 18.29 percent).[16]

The roots of houselessness in the District spread wide and run deep.

In 1984 Initiative 17, the DC Right to Overnight Shelter Act (often referred to as the right to shelter law) passed with an overwhelming 72 percent of the vote, making DC one of the first in the country to legislate a legal right to shelter. It guaranteed "safe, sanitary, and accessible shelter space, offered in an atmosphere of reasonable dignity" for the District's unhoused. However, for more than four years after the law passed, District officials largely ignored it. Instead of establishing new shelter spaces, they took shortcuts and set up mobile trailers in government-owned parking lots in the Northeast neighborhoods of Trinidad and Brentwood. Some of the places where cots were placed included the gyms of in-use schools, a rooming house with no heat and broken windows, the Robert F. Kennedy Memorial Stadium dressing rooms—including the one used by the Washington Football Team cheerleaders—and the DC Council building.[17]

Following a lengthy trial in January 1989, Superior Court judge Harriet Taylor found the city to be in clear violation of the law. During the trial, unhoused people and health workers testified that shelter residents were forced to use blankets so filthy the staff wouldn't touch them and that the shelters were infested with rats, lice, and scabies. Streams of running sewage flowed through some buildings from toilets left broken for months at a time, and in one shelter in upper Northwest, more than 150 men were housed in a space designed for 61.

In her decision, Judge Taylor noted that the city's shelters were grossly overcrowded, filthy, and unsafe, summarizing them as "virtual hell-holes."[18] Taylor issued a preliminary injunction ordering the city to increase shelter capacity and improve safety and sanitation conditions in existing shelters. In April of the same year, District officials voluntarily signed a consent decree that spelled out the city's obligations to provide emergency shelter, agreeing to open additional facilities as needed and to maintain reasonable health and safety standards. Many people, including DC Council member Nadine Winter, opposed the decision. Winter quickly introduced an amendment the same month that set out to limit shelter use to ten days per six-month period, publicly stating, "We have done what we can to make them human beings"[19] in reference to people who were unhoused.

In July of 2019, I searched for this quote over a period of several days. I had a vague recollection of reading it somewhere years earlier, but could not recall where, what the exact wording was, or even who exactly said it, but I became obsessed with finding it. I eventually discovered it cited in an April 2019 article[20] by a postdoctoral research fellow at Georgetown. By my best recollections, I had originally seen the quote on a blog maintained by an unhoused person living in DC who created his posts semiregularly at a DC Public Library computer. I had been horrified by Winter's words then, and I am horrified by them now. But where they were public and blatant in their cruelty, much of DC's policy decisions and stances in recent years are more covert and glossed over, and I don't know which is worse.

In 2005, the Right to Overnight Shelter Act was officially removed from the legal code and replaced with the Homeless Services Reform Act, which is still in place today. One of the main governances of the act is that there is a legal right to shelter during hypothermia season. In 2018 alone, the District spent $25 million to shelter families in motels. When the temperature is below freezing, temporary shelters are opened. When temperatures rise again, hundreds of people are left without access to overnight shelter once more.

All of this goes hand in hand with how Northwest One became a hub for unhoused people. In 2017, when the central Martin Luther King Jr. Memorial Library closed, the patrons who had considered it a community center and daily refuge were displaced. The next-closest libraries to MLK, the easiest to walk to, were the Shaw Library (1.1 miles from MLK) and Northwest One (1.0 miles from MLK). A few days after the planned closing, a senior official in the DC Department of Human Services told the *Washington Post*: "I think we could have handled this a lot better. Maybe in our own way we kinda kept putting it off. It's probably one of the hardest things we'd had to endure as a department in terms of serving the homeless. The library was such a strong foundation of the [homeless] services provided."[21]

The library was never officially a part of the city's homeless services. There was no partnership, agreement, or formal contract. The hundreds of unhoused patrons who arrived at its doors every morning by bus from the shelters would imply otherwise, but librarians knew better: there was an unspoken, informal agreement that they always had, and would continue, to fill in the gaps of services and resources for unhoused people.

7

FOR WHOM

If you are used to being seen as a public nuisance, why bother tiptoeing in imaginary slippers through the hallowed halls of venerable institutions?

—Maria Tumarkin, *Axiomatic*

IN MY FIRST MONTH AT THE BRANCH, there were four incident reports filed, in addition to the one on my first day. There were also hundreds of undocumented interactions between patrons, and between workers and patrons, that were less than positive, but official incident reports were filed only when a patron was barred from the library or the police had been involved.

The second incident report filed in January was on the eighteenth and had been handled at the branch level without involving Library or Metropolitan Police. Frank warned a regular patron about not sleeping in the library by waking him and handing him one of the blue Library Rules of Behavior pamphlets, in which he had highlighted the rule that prohibited "Lying down, sleeping, or the appearance of sleeping on the premises." The rule advised that "Sitting Customers must use library-provided seating (chair, couch, etc.). Customers may not sit on the floor, sidewalk, etc. unless approved by a library staff member and may not block aisles, exits, pathways, or entrances." The patron rubbed his eyes, took the blue pages, and wearily responded that he would remember for the future.

I was taught to wake sleeping patrons like him by gently knocking on the table near them. While knocking I would say, "Sir?" or "Ma'am?" or their first name if I knew it. If the patron moved, I'd gently ask, "You doing OK?" until they responded in some form. If it was impossible to wake someone from sleep, we called paramedics to provide medical care. But a grumble or movement meant they were alive, and this was when I was supposed to remind them that they couldn't sleep in the library.

I used to fall asleep at a study carrel on the fifth floor of the Lockwood Memorial Library on the University at Buffalo campus frequently in undergrad and then again in graduate school. The carrels had cushioned benches with built-in desk lamps that created a soft, warm light. In the frigid Buffalo winters the heat would be blasting and I'd settle in to do work and end up falling asleep on a pile of books and printed pages instead. No one ever woke me up—not a librarian or a campus security guard. I am sure they had rules about sleeping too, but they weren't enforced against me. I was not sleeping there out of necessity, but if I had been woken by a stranger, I would have felt embarrassed, discombobulated, upset.

Regulars, especially those who slept in shelters or outside, were often exhausted from the hypervigilance that sleeping in a shelter or on the streets or in other unstable environments requires. They always remained physically and mentally prepared to keep themselves safe, but they also knew they had some elevated level of safety at the library. They knew that staff—or at the very least, video surveillance—would prevent an attack or their things being stolen without being able to identify the culprit. It was easy for me to understand how they fell asleep in the library, often without meaning to. Waking up adults who were clearly exhausted felt particularly patronizing and punitive, but then I would think about someone dying from intoxication, an overdose, or an underlying health concern because we didn't try, and I would stand up, walk over, and start knocking.

On January 22, 2018, Frank noticed the same patron from four days earlier sleeping again. When he was awake, the man had a big, gap-toothed smile and shoulder-length dreadlocks he kept off his face with a thick yellow bandanna. He was sometimes friendly, sometimes not, and it was impossible to predict when you would get what. When he came up to the circulation desk, it was usually to point out that the copy machine or a computer was reading his mind or someone was recording his thoughts without his permission. Sometimes he'd tap his temple and tell us they were recording our thoughts, too.

Frank walked over to where the man was sleeping and woke him. He asked his name, and the man told him it was Valiant Steele. On the library incident report that followed, Valiant Steele was listed as Black/African American, tall, and between the ages of thirty-five and forty-five. In a photograph attached to the report, his body is leaned against the side of a chair with a bandanna pulled down over his eyes. One arm is protectively crossed over his stomach; the other hand is wrapped around his hip. His long legs are extended out and crossed at the ankles. His body is slumped and adjusted to sleep as comfortably as possible in a position of complete surrender to exhaustion.

Whenever there was an incident, the report was e-mailed to all staff with at least one administrator cc'd. Often, we included the manager of the Shaw branch as well, as patrons who had been barred at Northwest One frequently walked the 0.9 miles over to Shaw, and vice versa. If a patron was barred from one branch, they were barred from visiting any of the DCPL branches as well. When I saw the photo of Valiant Steele attached to the e-mail I read the next morning, I thought of the many times I'd watched one of my uncles pass out at a holiday party after working the night shift as a delivery driver or firefighter, or after having one too many beers. They'd fall asleep on any surface—a kitchen chair, a couch, leaning against the wall—snoring quietly through the surrounding noise. Valiant's body looked like theirs did. I felt the same tenderness for him in that moment as I'd so often felt for the tired, overburdened men in my own family. Valiant was exhausted and had fallen asleep.

In the report, Frank wrote: "When I woke him up, I informed him that he was barred, and asked for his name, address and birthday. Valiant apologized and I told him that there are consequences for breaking the library rules. Valiant left without further incident." Valiant had been barred from the library for the rest of the day.

Those who spent the entirety of their days at the library knew most of the general library rules: no sleeping, no eating in the computer lab, keep your voice to a conversational level, don't use someone else's library card. They did their best to adhere, and we did our best to be understanding and flexible. I tried to imagine who made these rules, though. A team of administrators from downtown? A group of librarians?

The DC Public Library Rules of Behavior—thirty-one in total when I worked there—were nothing if not specific. They covered everything from headphone volume to engaging in sexual activity on library grounds. I was beginning to question, more and more, the many expectations we were holding so many different people to. This was also tangled up in the fact that the Board of Library Trustees was, and remains, the body responsible for approving the Library Rules of Behavior. They outline the many rules as policy intended to "provide and maintain a safe and secure environment in which every customer can obtain equitable access to information, expanded opportunities and an increased quality of life. The guidelines will act as rules of conduct for library customers, in order to deter and/or minimize the effect of unacceptable behavior, by defining such behavior so that individuals may conduct themselves in a manner consistent with the purpose and functions of DCPL." The chief librarian and executive director of DCPL is the official person to establish rules and, with assistance from his team of administrators, oversee the day-to-day operations of the library. But he could not be in all twenty-six branches at once. As far as I saw and knew, he mostly remained in his office on K Street with the other administrators.

Social norms exist on a spectrum. Not everyone behaves the same way, especially not people who have experienced trauma, as so many patrons at Northwest One had. Their actions, reactions, beliefs—their behaviors and ways of being in the world overall—were informed by this trauma, sometimes in ways others could readily understand, but often-times not. In libraries, expected norms are often outlined explicitly in policies and procedures handbooks and rulebooks. The hope in making these documents is that all library users and staff feel safe and comfort-able operating under clear and consistent boundaries for all—under clear, agreed-on norms. At their most effective, library rules help to eliminate profiling or biases. And in an ideal situation, the rules are enforced by library staff who are familiar with patrons in a way that is conducive to leniency and patience, and, if necessary, de-escalation. This is obviously not always the case. There are new patrons whom staff are not yet familiar with, patrons who could be suffering from mental illness, actions that are complicated by symptoms or behaviors that staff are not able to anticipate or adequately equipped to handle.

I knew from my work in the schools that people of all ages who have had unclear boundaries in the past may push against even the most clearly established boundaries to more clearly define them. I also knew that people who create, or are enforcing, rules often struggle to see it this way. Especially when the pushback is violent, as I saw on my first day and many more times in the months that followed.

Even with this basic understanding of, and patience for, trauma-impacted behavior, the reality was that I felt unsafe at the library every day. I was constantly mentally prepared for emergencies or crises or verbal assaults that were never really all that predictable. Every person who worked at Northwest One was experiencing some level of this same hypervigilance we witnessed in so many of our patrons. My coworkers who had worked at the branch for more than five years, all Black women, had learned to compartmentalize, ignore, and deflect. Jackie was the most likely to yell back at patrons, sometimes escalating situations, especially with patrons who were having delusions or other symptoms of mental illnesses. Ms. Olson and Ms. Williams were mostly calm and chose not to react most of the time. This had shocked me in the beginning. Ms. Williams, especially, would repeat, "You can't let them get to you" when she saw me getting upset about something that was happening. But I knew it got to her too. I saw how her entire body ached, how she would slightly remove a headphone to hear what a patron was yelling and shake her head back and forth, saying, "Mm, mm, mmmm." How she, too, left the circulation desk to go into the back room for an early lunch some days and had to walk away from patrons, tagging in a coworker with a line we all used: "I can't do it today."

I knew I was not the first person to work at Northwest One to vocalize concerns about the many issues at the branch. But the help we had all at one point or another asked for rarely came, and the concerns we rightly raised were often met with canned replies. In meetings, administrators in the DC Public Library system had told me that the Northwest One branch was an outlier, an anomaly, an exception—one of two or three others within the system whose circulation statistics were low while numbers of people through the door were exponentially higher. Whose visitors were almost exclusively experiencing combinations of house-lessness, extreme poverty, addiction, and mental health issues. In one meeting where I spoke up, the administrator in charge had said, "Your branch is unique." And in some ways it was, but this had more to do with the neighborhood it was in than anything else.

In the spring of 2018, three garter snakes were found at the George-town library branch, located in one of the wealthiest parts of DC. The branch closed for three days, and the story was featured in the *Washington Post* with the headline A D.C. LIBRARY WAS CLOSED FOR MORE THAN TWO DAYS AFTER SEVERAL LIVE SNAKES WERE FOUND INSIDE.[1] The snakes were small and a completely common and harmless species. The article states: "Not wanting to reopen until the building was snake-free, the library remained closed for two more days—until the pest-control company declared the area clear."

By August of 2018, Northwest One had had at least four bedbug "incidents" since my start date of January 8. Two of those times, my coworkers and I discovered them because we found them crawling on us. It was in our government contracts that we would not be compensated for any damages incurred by a bedbug infestation in our private homes. When there were bedbugs I would return home and put $1.50 worth of quarters into one of the building's machines to wash my clothes and another $1.50 in quarters to dry them at the highest setting, hoping I had killed the bugs. I bleached the bottoms of my shoes at the end of every shift, ruining several pairs, and I threw out entire outfits that couldn't be machine washed.

The official procedure for when we found a bedbug was to call "down-town" to report it to the library administrator on duty. We were required to isolate the bug—catching it on a piece of tape or underneath a clear cup—and eventually, an employee from Orkin would come and verify that it was indeed a bedbug. Only when it was identified were we allowed to close the branch for the day. Sometimes this process took upward of three hours, and we always, without fail, opened the following day. The separation between the administrators who made the important calls of whether a branch closed and the employees who intimately knew the buildings they worked in and patrons they served grew wider and wider in my view as weeks and months went by. I eventually requested Freedom of Information Act (FOIA) documents about bedbug treatments at libraries across the city. All the branches with bedbugs were in neighborhoods of DC with the highest poverty rates. No one had written a *Post* article about them. No one seemed to care.

———————

You would be hard-pressed to enter a library anywhere in the United States that does not have marginalized and vulnerable groups who regularly patronize it. You need only ask the librarians who work there for confirmation. Unless you don't want to hear it. Unless you want to ignore it, place the onus on employees, and keep supporting systems that push marginalized groups farther and farther away, to some new town or city, to some new library, as so many library administrators do, unconsciously and consciously.

The DCPL administrators' responses implied several things. The most infuriating, to me, was that they clearly wanted to gloss over what they had falsely categorized as problems specific to only a few branches, including Northwest One. Their attention—their energy and money and programs—would go to the "other" branches, ones that they felt they could help. Ones in "better" neighborhoods. I saw this attitude of putting money into branches that were easier to help—and better to showcase—reflected prominently in the blueprints for the MLK library modernization. As the central library in the DC Public Library system and being located in the epicenter of downtown DC, MLK unquestionably served unhoused populations, perhaps more than any other location in the system. But the designs for it reflected who the $211 million renovations were envisioned for and most benefited. The blueprints were released publicly in 2018, and I saw that there were plans for a rooftop terrace, a sculptured staircase, a large auditorium and conference center, and maker spaces for fabrication, music production, and art. These were beautiful, modern additions to a community space that would certainly benefit and delight many, but I mostly saw what and who was missing from these designs. A truly innovative library system would have considered adding free storage lockers, public showers, a clean needle exchange, and other spaces designated to provide community outreach and care—especially at its central branch that so clearly served vulnerable populations, including the people who arrived by multiple buses from the shelters every morning and the many unhoused people who slept against the building's walls.

DC is not alone in these decisions that cater, at least on a surface level, to tourists and the middle and upper classes. There is the New York City Public Library Stephen A. Schwarzman Building, often referred to as the city's central branch, on Fifth Avenue and West Forty-Second Street whose Rose Main Reading Room is officially a New York City landmark and the shooting location of dozens of well-known movies. Expensive renovations were made to the library's Rose Reading Room in 2016, improving its fifty-two-foot-tall ceilings and cloud murals.

There are the eleven stories of the Seattle Public Library's steel and glass central branch, with architectural and design surprises like the fourth-floor Red Hall made of bloodred curving walls and walkways that are popular in Instagram photos.

The Main Library of the San Francisco Public Library system opened at its current site in 1996 at a cost of more than $122 million, and it features seven floors with a dramatic skylight in the building's five-story central atrium. Bridges connect the floors across light wells, and a staircase rises four stories.

The Boston Public Library's Central Library in Copley Square looks much the same as it did when it opened in 1895 and was declared a "palace for the people," with Renaissance Revival architecture, arches, coffered ceilings, and neat rows of wooden tables with green glowing reading lamps at each.

Each of these central branches is large—they have the most space, seating, and bathrooms—and attract larger numbers of people. All of them have at least some systems in place to support marginalized groups, but the buildings themselves do not reflect this care. Instead, they imply a level of grandeur not unlike the ones wealthy White men first wanted to provide to the public in the earliest days of public libraries in America.

Many public libraries across the country still exist in historic buildings like these, and money is, time and time again, put into their upkeep and restoration. And the DC Public Library is hardly the first major library system in the country to redesign branches without keeping marginalized groups in mind. It does not have to be, and *should not* be, this way.

Beyond my concerns about the blueprints I had seen for MLK, I was full of other, more pressing, questions related to the library: How could administrators disregard their employees so easily? How could we be asked to provide so much with so little understanding, support, or training? How could I protect myself and protect others and not dissolve into constant fear? How had library school not prepared me for any of this? How could so many people so badly need help and not receive it?

The more questions I had, the more it felt like there was an empty black void I was asking them into. I had no idea how wide or deep it went and was beginning to not want to find out. I didn't feel like yelling and not being heard anymore. I didn't have the energy or the emotions I'd had when I was first hired. No one at Northwest One did. And we all stood on the edge of this unknown and dark space. We teetered on it, shifting our weight between losing our cool on patrons, or each other, and quitting altogether. We tried to maintain some sort of balance on the lip, and it was a constant, daily effort to not fall.

For Frank, it was Valiant Steele who pushed him over the edge.

With three hours left before the branch closed for the day, Frank had been working on the photocopier. We'd recently switched to a policy of free printing, but the machine had continued to charge people. It had been the bane of all our days as patrons had a range of near-constant reactions to it. Some simply asked whether they really still had to pay, and others stood in the center of the library where the machine was and shouted, "You fucking told me this was free now! You lied to me!" On each of our desk shifts we had fielded these questions, at varying levels of volume and annoyance, in addition to the normal work of the day. I was thrilled that we had switched to free printing, but the first few weeks of its rollout had been less than smooth.

There had been a lull in new people coming into the branch for the night, and Frank was using the time to see what he could fix in the copier's settings. Valiant Steele was at the table just behind him, watching his every movement with an even deeper skepticism of the technology than normal. He very deeply believed that an FBI or CIA agent controlled the copier and used it to mess with him.

I had asked my therapist for appropriate ways to respond to patrons in moments like these. She had told me I could say things like, "That sounds really scary, I'm sorry" or "That must be very frightening, is there anything I can help you with right now?" I hadn't worked out the best way to respond to Valiant's accusations against the copier yet, but he had been becoming more and more obsessed with it.

When Valiant had started speaking to Frank that day, he'd been completely calm. From my chair behind the circulation desk, I couldn't hear what either of them was saying, nor was I paying much attention. But I noticed Frank was the first to raise his voice.

"Well, you can't film me, so I'm going to need you to leave here right now."

I looked over to see what Valiant was holding, confused as to when he might have secured a cell phone or camera, but there was nothing in his hands. He was in his seat, smiling his mischievous smile at Frank.

"You need to get out of here. It is illegal to film me!"

Frank was yelling now in a way I had never seen before. His face and the top of his head were bright red. Chris made a movement to walk over, but I grabbed his arm. I knew the more people who got involved, the more upset both Frank and Valiant might get. We watched from the circulation desk, ready to intercede if necessary. Eventually, Frank stormed into the back office, and Valiant got up and left, smiling at Chris and me with his arms bent at his waist and his shoulders shrugged as if to say, *What did I do?*

A few minutes later Frank was back out on the floor with his hat and messenger bag on. There were still three hours left in his shift.

"I'm leaving for the day," he explained.

I had never seen him so upset. Valiant had told Frank he was filming him, and when Frank turned to see how, Valiant tapped his left temple and said, "I'm filming you with my eyes." It is a testament to the mental and emotional erosion we all experienced at Northwest One that Frank snapped. He was at the end of his patience for these kinds of interactions, and while I could criticize that, I also deeply understood. He had gone over the proverbial edge.

The next day, all staff received an e-mail telling us that he had been reassigned to a new branch and we would be receiving an interim manager. Frank was the first of three managers I had in my nine months at the branch.

After Frank left Northwest One, we got Robert. Robert was from a rural Virginia town, had an affinity for Dolly Parton and Delta Burke, and brought a deep, and deeply needed, level of humor back into the space. He could turn most situations at the circulation desk into positive conversations, and I rarely saw him become fazed. When patrons yelled, he'd smile slightly and listen until they were done, then coolly respond. When a female patron came in wearing a T-shirt and no pants or underwear and sat down at a computer in the computer lab, he went inside and said, "Ma'am, until you have pants on, we need you to leave for the day, OK? We'll be happy to have you back when you have pants on." He handed her a packet of information we had put together with a list of nearby shelters, showers, and other resources, and waited for her to respond. In interactions with other staff, this same woman often yelled, but with Robert she would laugh, smile, and say, "All right, all right. I know." His genuine kindness and sense of humor were agreeable to almost everyone. Robert was, and still is, one of my favorite people (he too has since left DCPL).

Shortly after Robert's hiring, I attended another meeting between library administrators and other children's and teen services librarians. These meetings were being called to create more transparency between "downtown"—our general term for the administrators who worked outside of branches in an office building on K Street NW—and library workers. Library technicians, library associates, and adult librarians each had their own grouped meetings that the library system wanted us to begin to have more regularly.

What I remember most about the meeting is what we did not discuss. When we were given time to ask questions at the end, I raised my hand and waited to be called on by the smiling woman in a neat business suit who had been in her role for just over a month. When she called on me, squinting at my name tag, I tried to keep my voice steady.

"We haven't spoken about homeless people this entire meeting. Or people struggling with their mental health or addiction."

She asked what branch I was from, and when I responded, a look of understanding crossed her face. I kept going.

"I wish we had spent some time talking about these individuals. If these are the people we are serving, we need to focus on them. We need training; we need help." I tried to speak deliberately, to choose my next words carefully. "It is traumatic to try to help people we aren't adequately equipped to help day after day. I can do my own research and find information, but I'm also tired at the end of the day, and the last thing I want to do is go home and spend additional time trying to figure out how to do more. If this is all part of the job, and for me it's a significant part, we need to talk about it in these meetings, too. We need to talk about the actual people we serve on a daily basis."

I finished and knew my face was flushed. The woman from downtown was staring at me, and I could also feel the eyes of my colleagues on me. It was silent for a few long seconds, but when I finally looked around the room, I saw that two librarians were close to crying. I had my hands clasped in my lap, knuckles white, readying myself for her response.

The woman finally spoke. "Yes, we're working on what to do with Northwest One."

Robert was eventually replaced with a permanent manager named Rose. Rose had been working for the DC Public Library for years, and she brought a level of empathy to the work that anyone who worked alongside her learned from. Rose didn't shy away from difficult conversations, and above all else, she valued maintaining positive relationships with patrons.

Around the same time that Rose was hired, we were assigned a full-time, gun-carrying Library Police officer named Officer Jones. This was the solution the woman from downtown had alluded to in the meeting. All the staff knew Officer Jones, and most regular patrons already knew him too. Many on staff called him Jonesy. He'd circulated between several nearby branches for years and chatted in equal amounts with staff and patrons. He was also one of four officers who had regularly responded to emergency calls at Northwest One. In his midfifties, Jonesy was one of the oldest officers the library employed. He was gentle and soft spoken and seemed to genuinely care about others. Jonesy became the one to intervene when patrons had mental health crises, drank and passed out, made verbal threats, or did any of the many other things that had normally been responded to by a collective effort by staff and, sometimes, a call to either, or both, Library Police and the DC Metropolitan Police Department.

Jonesy preferred to sit directly across from the circulation desk in a chair in the children's area. Sometimes, just as a patron began to raise their voice, he'd shout, "Hey!" and the patron would stop immediately. Every half hour or so, he would rise from his chair and walk around the library, doing things like waking up and checking on sleeping patrons, ensuring no one stayed in the bathroom for too long, and defusing arguments. Our daily incidents immediately became less frequent after Jonesy was brought on, and my job became, in the simplest word, *easier*. The first week he was at our branch was the first week since my first day that I wasn't verbally assaulted or sexually harassed by a patron. My relief was immense, but so were my guilt, anger, and confusion. I was glad to no longer have so much enforcement and surveillance be my responsibility, but I was also disturbed that this monitoring was now being done by someone who carried a gun.

The DC Public Library has hired and employed gun-carrying police officers since at least 1978,[2] in part because DC public libraries are considered DC government property, the same as the Capitol, the Lincoln Memorial, and so forth. In 2018, DCPL assigned individual officers to eight of the District's branches, including Northwest One, and each of the branches also served predominantly BIPOC and/or high-poverty populations and neighborhoods. (New Orleans Public Library employs gun-carrying police officers as well. So does the Fulton County Library System, which includes Atlanta. It is no coincidence that these cities have Black populations upward of 50 percent.)

I got to know four of the twenty-five Library Police officers employed by DCPL well. I saw them often. I knew where they had grown up, what sports teams they loved, and which lunch spots nearby were their favorites. I bought Girl Scout Cookies from their children, and we shared snacks and stories and jokes in the back office or at the circulation desk on slow days. All the officers I knew well and saw frequently were Black, including Jonesy, and several of them had previously worked for the NYPD. They were all outwardly kind, and many of them were excellent at de-escalating situations, especially with library patrons struggling with addiction or their mental health. None, to my knowledge, had ever discharged the guns they carried on their hips while working for the library. They were often overextended as well, though they had received more formal training in their work and were practiced at responding to what came their way.

Former Dallas police chief David Brown was praised in a 2016 *New York Times* piece for earning "a national reputation as a progressive leader whose top priority is improving relations and reducing distrust between the police department and the city's minority residents."[3] Brown, who now serves as Chicago's police superintendent, has regularly spoken candidly about the nature of police work. Some of his perspective is informed by his own lived experiences, including losing his son in a June 2010 police shooting, seven weeks into his position as Dallas's chief. His son, David Brown Jr., suffered from bipolar disorder and had been exhibiting psychotic and paranoid behavior in the days leading up to the incident, in which he shot and killed a Lancaster, Texas, police officer. Brown Jr. was subsequently shot more than a dozen times by other responding officers.

Dallas's crime rates fell to fifty-year lows while Brown led the department in reforms that included reducing the use of force, increasing transparency, and equipping officers with body cameras. At a news conference in July 2016, Chief Brown stated: "We're asking cops to do too much in this country. We are. Every societal failure, we put it off on the cops to solve. Not enough mental health funding, let the cops handle it. . . . Schools fail, let's give it to the cops. . . . That's too much to ask. Policing was never meant to solve all those problems."[4]

I see many of the frustrations librarians feel echoed here. It is not that librarians and libraries don't want to do some of the work; it is that they, too, can't do much of what is often "put off" on them. I struggle with seeing similarities and echoes of my own feelings in these statements, as library work is distinctly different, removed from, even in direct opposition to police work. But there were levels of enforcement, surveillance, protection, reaction, and overreaction at the library also. We had surveillance cameras around the library, we enforced the Rules of Behavior, we filed incident reports, we responded to the urgent needs and struggles of community members, and we eventually employed someone who carried a gun.

In order to make Northwest One feel "safe," to be able to keep it open and operating, the library had relied on a police presence to most quickly "fix" it. And in many real ways, it did change some of the more frightening or unsafe aspects of the library for employees and patrons. Many regular patrons at the branch also wanted fewer violent incidents, fewer arguments, and more quiet. But hiring the officers also did very little, if not nothing, to address the systemic issues in the neighborhood and few, if any, of the pressing individual issues of the patrons who were struggling the most.

Public libraries all around the country are trying, with some success, to address many of the existing social gaps in more pointed ways. One of the more recent and innovative actions has been the introduction of librarian social workers. In 2009, the San Francisco Public Library hired Leah Esguerra as the nation's first full-time librarian social worker. Esguerra oversees a team of formerly unhoused people who provide peer counseling and outreach at branches around the city. Many other library systems in the country followed suit, including the DC Public Library, which hired Jean Badalamenti in May of 2014. Badalamenti is consistently cited in news stories as "social worker," but her official title is "manager, health and human services," as her social worker license was expired in 2014 and, as of 2020, still is.

Badalamenti's hiring was largely a direct response to the District's losing 50 percent of its affordable housing between 2003 and 2015. Her position was meant to help with the subsequent uptick in library services utilized and needed. Similar to Esguerra, Badalamenti began working with peer outreach groups to serve DC Public Library branches. Public libraries all over the country hoped bringing in social workers would help them make library spaces more comfortable for all.

In March of 2018, Badalamenti set up twice-weekly visits to North-west One with a peer outreach team of formerly unhoused people. When she and two peer workers arrived on the first day, they quickly realized there was no private space in which patrons could meet with them. Only two patrons were willing to publicly sit with the peer outreach team that first day, and as far as I saw, no more than a half dozen people ever did. We tried to encourage our patrons to talk to them—some we had been speaking to about their services for days in advance—but the peer work-ers mostly remained alone at the tables, talking to each other. There was perhaps discomfort about new faces or anger at the entire table they took up, but I suspected the key factor was the discomfort or embarrassment of being forced to so publicly seek help.

Many efforts by libraries and librarians to address the more systemic causes of social gaps similarly involve a level of trial and error and a delib-erate, sometimes lengthy, process to build trust within the community—as they should, I would argue, but the progress is not rapid enough to keep up with so much human need. Badalamenti and her team did the best they could with the month they had. Their actions and the resources they were offering were well researched, noble, and entirely free, but patrons at Northwest One had their own reasons for not trusting or seeking their help. There was not enough time to build the necessary trust, and at the end of the month, they had to move on to the next library.

It is much easier to provide library services to people whose basic needs are already met. Public meeting spaces, author events, book clubs, story times, movie rentals, and programming geared toward community interests are some of the many services most libraries offer in person more readily and regularly. It is the offerings and initiatives that would address more systemic problems, ones not directly within the stated mission of the library, that often require more money, effort, energy, and time. It is understandable that an institution often manned in the day-to-day by overextended library workers might focus their time and energy on these more achievable goals of outreach and community first and, also, most often. I believe it is the responsibility of all librarians to think more broadly than this, but it is absolutely the responsibility of administrators (and community leaders, library board members, and others who make most decisions around money and training) to provide the tools—in whatever forms—to make that work more possible and prevalent. Any sort of fundamental and systemic change that develops within libraries and extends out to the communities they serve depends on this, more than anything that individual librarians can do on their own.

8

BURNING OUT

Only a fire can teach you what survives a fire. No, it teaches you what can survive that fire.

—Sarah Manguso, *300 Arguments*

DURING THE SPRING MONTHS, Northwest One's computer lab closed for three hours every Tuesday and Thursday evening for a free, basic computer skills class. This was some of the only adult programming the branch offered, and it was well attended. During one of these evening classes, a regular patron came in to work on a job application and was told by staff that he would have to come back the next day when the lab was open to the public again. He became upset, and the conversation escalated enough that someone on staff called Library Police.

Neither Rose nor I had been working, but I listened the next day as she spoke firmly to all the employees about what had passed. "Someone should have listened to what he was saying and helped him. He could have sat in one of the empty computers at the back of the class, no problem, and someone should have realized and allowed that. This is a relationship we may never be able to repair."

This was the kind of conversation I had longed for, especially when I first started at the branch: one where we were encouraged to extend genuine kindness and understanding to patrons who came to ask for reasonable help, rather than ignoring or denying them. I expected to feel thrilled by the silence of the collective resonance that followed—for once, no one on staff pushed back—but I was numb instead. *It's too late now*, I thought. I knew the patron would likely not come back to the branch—not after that.

In that moment, I realized it didn't just seem too late for the patron, but it seemed too late for Northwest One overall. I didn't see a pathway where we got better support, better training, better helping tools. I didn't see a future where it got better or easier, for staff or for visitors to the branch. It didn't seem possible to have a future where administrators didn't brush off what employees tried to communicate in meetings and on the online message board they'd set up called the Water Cooler, where stories and grievances were openly aired for all to see. I didn't see a future where DC did more and better for its most vulnerable people, either.

During the years I was a librarian, I operated around the word *empathy*. It was something of a defense mechanism in library work, and oftentimes it was my best one. In Leslie Jamison's profound book of essays, *The Empathy Exams*, she writes: "Empathy isn't just listening, it's asking the questions whose answers need to be listened to. Empathy requires inquiry as much as imagination. Empathy requires knowing you know nothing. Empathy means acknowledging a horizon of context that extends perpetually beyond what you can see."[1]

On the flip side, there is some research that people are more empathetic toward individuals who resemble themselves, and this can potentially exacerbate social inequalities. In my practiced interpretation of the word *empathy*, I tried, always, to respond to others with some understanding of who they were as a human being with unique experiences and perspectives that I could never fully understand. I worked from a willingness and desire to learn at least parts of what I did not know, in hopes that it would make it easier for me to understand, or deal with, difficult interactions. My intense focus on empathy—in being empathetic—is part of what made me a decent librarian, but it is also a significant part of why I burned out so spectacularly.

I didn't learn the term *empathy fatigue* until well after I left Northwest One. The term was first coined as *compassion fatigue* in a 1992 piece by oncology nurse Carla Joinson, who wrote about the emotional, physical, and psychological impacts of working in her field.[2] It is perhaps best defined as a state of tension and preoccupation with the individual or cumulative traumas of people whom someone serves. Though the term has been embraced by much of the psychological community, it has not yet been included in the *Diagnostic and Statistical Manual of Mental Disorders.*

I would define empathy fatigue as the physically and emotionally painful and complicated consequence of repeated exposure to stressful or traumatic events. It most often results from working directly with victims of disasters, trauma, or illness. Social workers, health-care workers, firefighters, journalists, teachers, and librarians are all particularly susceptible to experiencing it.

I was strangely comforted when I learned how many other terms there were in addition to *empathy fatigue*: compassion fatigue, secondary traumatic stress (STS), vicarious traumatization, vocational awe. Each term embodies the same sets of common symptoms and behaviors that manifest both emotionally and physically: numbness and disconnect, isolating from others, feeling angry, sad, depressed; feeling speechless or unable to respond appropriately to what's happening around you; a lack of energy; headaches, nausea, changes in appetite; inability to concentrate; self-medication with drugs and/or alcohol.[3] Each term meant someone, or someones, had tried to find a way to give voice to the symptoms that made people feel like they were drowning and, ultimately, deluged into someone less caring, less well, less able.

In the workplace, empathy fatigue can look like a nurse refusing to admit someone clearly experiencing withdrawal symptoms to the detox unit at a hospital because it's about to close. It can be a hospital clerk having no reaction to a deceased man's grieving family as they try to figure out how to pay their bill. It is a doctor stoically telling a devastated family member they cannot see a gunshot wound victim because the emergency room is too busy. It is a librarian calling a homeless shelter to see if there is vacancy for a patron and telling the patron there isn't any and that they need to help the next person in line now. Almost always, empathy fatigue results in difficulty continuing to care.

It is easy to see how empathy fatigue—a condition that embodies so many symptoms and behaviors—can have ripple effects in places of employment. Chronic absenteeism, high staff turnover rates, friction between employees and employer, and increases in workers' compensation claims are chronic in environments where empathy fatigue is common. Another impact of empathy fatigue within organizations is a culture of silence, where stressful events are not discussed in their aftermaths. This happened often at Northwest One. In the wake of even the most violent or upsetting incidents, we rarely discussed the personal impacts they had on us. We took a long lunch break, slammed the office door, went home at the end of a shift, and tried to compartmentalize. We also tried to remind each other to "take care of yourself," but I don't think any of us knew quite what this looked like in practice.

After my first few months at Northwest One, I struggled to think clearly or gather my thoughts when speaking. I began ignoring friends' invitations, preferring to spend time alone on my couch watching Netflix where I knew no one would talk to or need me. There was not exactly relief in knowing this, but a few checked-out hours of not being constantly hypervigilant or panicked that someone might need me became essential. My muscles ached constantly, and I had chronic migraines that no medication was helping.

I also felt all of it in my spirit, which is to say the parts of me that existed beyond my thinking brain and body. My abilities to have perspective or optimism were almost nonexistent, like some core part of me had darkened to a point where I could not collect any of the kindness or patience or drive that I once had. I was constantly either numb or trying to be numb.

At work, I was beginning to feel nothing in response to even the most upsetting situations. In the spring of 2018, my therapist, Susan, gently started to speak to me about my mental health and a potential diagnosis. For months, I had talked with her about the insomnia I was experiencing and the nightmares I had most nights. In one recurring nightmare, a regular patron locked himself in the bathroom, died, and then came back to haunt the branch. In each iteration, I tried different ways to help him process his pain so that he could pass over, and every single time I failed. He returned again and again. I had another repeated nightmare about a patron who in waking life had drunkenly shouted that I was "his baby" and tried to come behind the circulation desk to touch me. In the nightmare, he got to me.

When I didn't have nightmares, it was because I barely slept or slept in short fits.

Susan knew the full scope of my social isolation and emotional detachment. She was familiar with the irritability and hypervigilance that prevented me from feeling comfortable around even my closest friends. She had seen the sensitivity I had developed to loud noises that were common in a busy city, the overwhelming desire I had to curl up into the fetal position and stay there, the ways I was shutting down.

I felt like a ticking time bomb when I wasn't at work. I could hold it mostly together there because it was my job and I knew I had to, at least to a degree, but I had no patience for people outside Northwest One. If someone didn't move to the right on a Metro escalator—something I had usually smiled over in the past—I yelled. If a friend wanted to tell me about something they were going through, I ignored their text messages or calls. If they tried to check in to ask how my day was, I had no idea how to begin to unpack how that day was without the context of what had happened the day and week before, but that had also been bad and unknown to them. When I tried to draft a response, I became relentlessly angry, thinking of how much cushier my friend's day-to-day was than mine. One friend finally visited me briefly at the branch and wrote afterward to tell me, "I think I understand now. I'm so sorry." I didn't know how to respond to that either.

Susan knew all the things I had been too embarrassed or confused by to admit to others. She had been patient when I canceled appointments again and again because I had another migraine or could not handle talking to her or anyone else. All of it, she explained at an appointment I finally showed up to, were symptoms and behaviors of someone experiencing not just empathy fatigue, but PTSD. Part of me felt relieved when she said those four letters—like I had proof of what was happening and how bad it felt. But part of me was also mortified. I had a warm apartment, a safe place to sleep, a reliable vehicle, friends, support—how could I claim the same diagnoses as some of my patrons? But this was one of the symptoms as well: I no longer had perspective. I no longer had the wherewithal to recognize what was happening to me. I didn't have the energy to care for myself, or to care about caring for myself, and I was struggling to care for my patrons by that point too.

I began to emulate some of the behaviors I had seen from other coworkers—days that Jonesy wasn't there, I blinked back in silence if a patron made an inappropriate comment or called me a bitch (or any number of the many things I was called), and I started to tell people, "No, this is ours" when they asked to borrow things like a stapler or highlighter. I stopped caring when the patron bathroom ran out of paper towels or toilet paper midway through a day and became annoyed instead. I knew by then that patrons were using the supplies to dry off after bathing or, as was the case with at least one regular patron, to soak paper towels in water and sit for a half hour making wet shapes on the floor with them. I felt increasingly emotionless when I told someone, "There is nothing I can do." I walked away from the circulation desk in the middle of a shift twice that summer, one of the times slamming the office door so hard I worried some part of it had broken. If I felt any emotion in my later months at Northwest One, it was anger. And not anger that was productive or noble and aimed at any social disparities—anger that festered and exploded.

I eventually received a formal diagnosis of complex PTSD. Where PTSD generally relates to a single event, complex PTSD is related to a series of events or one prolonged event. The diagnosis had roots years deep that had grown outside the library, but it was exacerbated, its symptoms multiplied, from working at Northwest One.

The actual work of being a public librarian, of showing up to that same building five days a week to perform an unending range of tasks in an environment that was unpredictable, chaotic, and sometimes violent, had warped everything in my life. If someone had told me ten years earlier when I first entered my MLS program that this would be the trajectory of my career, and that I would be diagnosed with complex PTSD in large part because of my work as a librarian, I don't think I would have believed them.

A coworker who had been at the branch longer than me received the same diagnosis a year later. I hadn't told them about my diagnosis, but I finally did when they reached out to tell me about theirs. Once I hit send on the text message, I watched the three dots of them writing a long reply and waited. What they finally sent back was short:

We didn't realize how bad it was.

We hadn't.

We knew how defeated and tired and depleted we felt, and we knew the numbness that had crept in too. We knew the toll the changes to our moods and behaviors had taken on our relationships and personal lives. We knew how frequently, but briefly, we talked to one another about how painful it often was, how helpless we felt. But we also knew we were doing the job we were expected to do and that people around us, especially the people in charge, knew how difficult it was. The managers, I suspect, felt just as helpless. The administrators made the major decisions and didn't seem to care enough to help, even when we asked, instead choosing to rely on the fact that we would show up, at a minimum, because we needed our paychecks. This disconnect often happens in hierarchal systems where "higher-ups" are detached from the daily work, and also, those administrators were right. Most of us stayed and did our jobs, for whatever personal reasons we had, up to and including wanting our paychecks. We stayed, and because we stayed many of us lost essential pieces of ourselves. As social scientist and professor Eve Ekman noted in 2011 when she was a crisis counselor and UC Berkeley research fellow conducting research on the impacts of empathy fatigue: "Many professionals used to burn out and leave their jobs. Now they burn out and stay."[4]

———————

Despite everything, I could still see a future where I continued working at the library. Where I eventually got transferred from Northwest One to an "easier" branch and my salary increased with a 3–5 percent bonus every year. Where I became more and more familiar with the patrons and melted away into a routine of tasks and interactions that I could manage mostly mindlessly, mostly numb, if I just shoved my feelings down enough. I knew that I could be decent at my job if I had to be but I might never have the energy or drive to make a *great* librarian, the kind who got awards or advocated for major changes within the field.

I saw that future—one of complacency and rote days and a deeper dive into numbness—and I knew I could do it. But I also knew every part of me did not want to.

The month before I started at Northwest One, I had submitted applications to creative writing MFA programs outside DC. I wanted to displace myself temporarily for the sake of a book I hoped to write about the concept of home, but by the time I had been working for a few months at Northwest One, I wanted to leave DC any way I could. I submitted the applications while I was still working in the schools, but when I accepted the position at Northwest One a month later I knew there was a possibility that I would be leaving it before a new year began.

I told myself that if I got rejection letters from every program, I would accept it as a sign that I should pour everything into being the best librarian I could be. But I also made a pact with myself that if I got an acceptance letter, I would give myself over completely to writing. I was at the library when I received the e-mail offering me a fully funded spot at the University of California, Riverside, for the creative writing MFA program's nonfiction cohort. By then Chris, Darrion, and Kenleigh all knew I had applied and we met up after work that evening to celebrate.

"You have to go," Darrion said. "You have to get out of here."

Despite the pact I had made with myself about moving forward with no regrets, I wavered.

My love for books since childhood, my belief that books and libraries had saved some part of me, is a beautiful way to explain why I became a librarian, but it was only one piece of the story that I had started to see more clearly at Northwest One. I became a librarian because I had been raised, not just by my family but by the socioeconomic class and religious beliefs and other established factors I was born into, with a mindset that to be a good person, it was my duty to help others. I became a librarian because I thought a helping career was all I could ever be good at, was all I could ever do to earn a paycheck that provided the financial stability I had always wanted. And by 2018, after working for nearly twenty years, I finally had some of that stability. There were a few hundred dollars left in my bank account at the end of the month, I took a vacation a couple of times a year, I had a car with payments I could afford, and I had a roof over my head. I had what I told myself I wanted during all those working years. But I had never checked back in with myself in adulthood about whether it was what I still wanted. I had never permitted myself to indulge in that kind of thinking.

I used whatever energy and self-care I had left to ask myself difficult questions: Was I really going to leave a career I had put so many years into? Was I going to stop working for the community I lived in? Would I trade financial stability for the uncertainty I had seen in so much of my childhood? Could I be that reckless, that *selfish*, with my life? I peeled back the answers like two pages I'd once found glued together by spilled soda in a returned library book. It was almost impossible to pull them apart, and even when I had finally separated them, there was no way to save those pages, no way to restore those words to readability.

There was no way I could look at my present and see a healthy future where I remained a librarian. No matter how deeply a hard-working, nose-to-the-grindstone attitude existed in my spirit, no matter how much I heard real and imagined voices saying, "You need a real job, with money," I could not choose the library. I could not continue to give and serve and advocate without completely losing myself, and deep down, I knew it.

The answer to all those tough questions was *yes*.

I gave Rose a month and a half's notice of my departure and decided to work until the last few days before my September 1 flight to Los Angeles. On my last day at Northwest One I arrived twenty minutes earlier than normal and sat at the circulation desk with the lights off to take in the space where I had spent most days of what felt like much longer than nine months. If a younger version of me were magically allowed a single snapshot of adulthood and was shown this—me, surveying an empty library from behind the circulation desk—she would be thrilled. Probably she would wonder how in the world one becomes a librarian and how I had, by the looks of things, become one. She would, I think, feel happy for me. But younger me would not understand the simultaneous grief and joy that snapshot held. How I was exiting one metaphorical road I had been on for over ten years and moving toward another.

Most major pieces of my life can be tied to two events: becoming a librarian and quitting library work. There were many, many side streets, but there were two roads after all, just like the famed Robert Frost poem has told us for generations. I suspect I am decades out from understanding the full magnitude of those two roads, but I knew when I left the library that the road away from it was one I might never navigate my way back to. And when I looked even farther back down the road I was exiting, to the optimistic determined woman in Buffalo who became a librarian, I recognized only that I wished I could have done, and cared, more for her.

Moving to California felt, in some ways, like a way to reclaim some selfish life for her.

On August 23, 2018, I signed out of Northwest One at 5:45 PM for the very last time. We still signed in and out of the branch by hand on a slip of paper, and I penned an exclamation point at the end of the time as Chris made a video of the moment. I hugged my coworkers. They wished me luck in California, and we got into our safety line of cars and drove away. I came home to an empty apartment: my belongings having been shipped off to the West Coast in a moving pod the day before, there was no furniture other than a rapidly deflating air mattress in my bedroom. I sat down in the middle of the hardwood floors of my living room and tightly hugged my knees to my chest, resting my chin on them.

For the first time in a very long time, I felt relief.

PART III

RECKONING

9

AN EDUCATION

Any story that cannot accommodate nuances is not interested in truth, but in obscuring it instead.

—Lacy M. Johnson, *The Reckonings*

IN MY EARLIEST CHILDHOOD UNDERSTANDING OF CALIFORNIA, it was far away, warm all the time, and everyone who lived there was tan, happy, and rich. I dreamed of California within the context of an almost unimaginable world where I would never again have a shovel in my hand or snow up to my knees and soaked socks, but instead would swim in the ocean every day between picking oranges from my orange tree and lemons from my lemon tree. In young adulthood, I imagined lives I could have had if one or two or ten things had gone differently, and California was often the backdrop. I envisioned a lush yard and weekends spent lounging in city parks, but all iterations of that life ultimately felt like an impossibility, a pipe dream, until I entered adulthood and came to understand that most things are possible with enough money. In the fall of 2018, I had a fellowship to cover my tuition and a few thousand dollars saved up in my savings account. Now that I was thirty-two years old, Southern California was finally a possibility.

The person I was when I started at Northwest One was different from the person who got on that 5:00 AM flight to Los Angeles and landed there in the early morning of September 1, jet lagged and excited. There was an almost instant softening when I exited the airport with my cat in a carrier and an air mattress zipped up in one of two suitcases. There were hulking mountains and swaying palm trees, warm weather and citrus trees—just like I'd remembered from two previous visits, just like I'd imagined when I was younger. All of it felt like it embodied my decision to leave libraries and focus on writing.

There would be joy here, I was certain, in the ways we often are when we exit one difficult environment and choose what we think, or hope, will be a better one. What was most important to me was that I felt a bit of optimism and hope again at all.

I settled into an apartment near the campus in Riverside and immediately began to fill my days with reading the stack of books that had been collecting on my bedside table in DC. I read them poolside in my apartment complex, watching the shadows the palm trees left on my body shift over hours, releasing some of the stress from the last few years. My body slowly began to catch up to my mind; my mind began to slowly catch up to my body. I was present, aware, *feeling* in the world again.

When the storage pod with all my belongings finally arrived, I unpacked articles of clothing I had only worn to work at the library. I had held on to them thinking I might still wear them somewhere, but I immediately bagged them up to be donated. I was trying in every way I could to compartmentalize those years, and I believed I was doing it in healthy ways this time. As I settled in, I thought about my aunt who had moved to California from the East Coast in her early twenties. She had always seemed fundamentally different from my other aunts and uncles who remained in Buffalo—freer and healthier and happier. I thought about what it meant to be from somewhere—both Buffalo and DC felt like home with a capital *H*—and what it meant to not just adapt, but thrive, outside that place.

My daily focus slowly shifted from care of others to care of self. From intensely focusing on how to be of service to whomever I encountered to making a two-year commitment to reading and writing. I was, I realized in those first months, beginning to allow the California I'd imagined in my childhood to become the California of my adulthood too. I was softer, warmer, slower. I was more self-centered, in the most generous sense of the word, than I had ever been before.

The first time I visited a public library in California was that first October. I had accepted a position as a grader for an undergraduate children's literature class a professor in my program was teaching. She had asked me to cover one of the lectures for her while she was out of town for an event, and the topic was one I knew well: how librarians select books to purchase for libraries. In preparation, I visited the main branch of the Riverside Public Library system to gather books that had a history of being banned. I wanted to begin the lecture by speaking to students about censorship, and I needed examples.

My experience going back to a library is hard to put words to, even now. I didn't know the space, but I also knew it exactly. The Riverside library had the same familiar rows of tall bookcases, same large-text signs marking different sections, same overhead lighting I'd come to despise and associate with migraines. The circulation desk was a half circle made of plywood, and the OPAC (online public access catalog) was on a stand-alone computer not far from it, just like at Northwest One. There were the same stained carpets soaking up years of lingering dust and body odor. There were the familiar black garbage bags of bedding and belongings tucked behind different structures of the building, partially hidden.

Upstairs, I was relieved to see the children's area was at least three times the size of the one I was most familiar with. I was after a few titles: *And Tango Makes Three*, *A Is for Activist*, *Tar Beach*, but none of them were on the shelves. I then quickly realized that what I was struggling to find were books that featured Black or Brown characters.

In 2019 Riverside's population was 53.7 percent Hispanic or Latino[1], but the shelves did not reflect this. I instinctively began to question who was ordering books: With what money? From whom? With what information at hand? Was someone who did not work directly with the public making purchasing decisions (this is not uncommon)? Were they reliant on donations or budget money or both? Were librarians purchasing books they found valuable without assessing circulation statistics? Without considering the community they served? Were most of the staff White?

I sat crouched on the ground in front of the short picture bookshelves, engaged in this thinking I was so familiar with, until one possible solution occurred to me. Maybe the books were simply checked out. I walked over to the circulation desk and gave the librarian title after title, but she responded, "No, we don't have that one" again and again in response. I eventually left the library with seven picture books, two of them featuring Black or Brown characters, and got into my car. As soon as I sat down, I started to cry. It was a defeated cry, not a productive one; it didn't end with any action plan or e-mails to the library manager. I was too disappointed and defeated, not just by the collection, but by being back in the familiar space of a library asking old questions about who and what the space was for.

The next night I stood at the front of a university classroom and propped the books I had collected on a table in front of me. As the forty or so students filed in I encouraged them to flip through the pages. I began the class by asking them to guess which of the titles had been challenged, or banned entirely, from school or public libraries. I saw humor and then confusion and anger pass over students' faces as I held up the books one by one and said, "This one too." Every book on the table was one that had been challenged. One incredulous student called out, "Why would people care about whether a penguin is gay?" as I explained the premise of *And Tango Makes Three*. They were as incensed as I hoped they might be, and I began the lecture.

Librarians with MLS degrees are often the main people responsible for purchasing the books for a library's collection, but different librarians and library systems, use different methodologies. The work often includes some combination of reading trade journals and blog posts from other librarians, following the work of popular authors, and using collection development data from general circulation statistics and then, perhaps, more involved information like population demographics.

In my years with the DC Public Schools, I skimmed the monthly *School Library Journal* and *American Libraries Magazine* copies that came in, using permanent marker to circle books I wanted to purchase whenever I received the yearly budget that during my tenure ranged from $1,000 to $10,000. I also kept an ongoing list at the circulation desk of books students requested. This was usually a joyful moment for students at checkout—asking for a new title and having it added to the list. I intended it to help students understand that the library was theirs and belonged to them, and that I was mostly there to guide them in using it. But school librarians were allowed to order only from specific vendors DCPS had contracts with, limiting the selections I could make even further. I could place book orders only once a year, and oftentimes I reached out to friends, family, and local businesses to donate or fund purchases of books on the student list.

At the public library, I was given a monthly budget to order books and mostly relied on my evolving sense of neighborhood demographics, circulation statistics, and bestseller numbers. An administrator for DCPL chose certain books each month that all libraries would receive as well. For the most popular releases, we were almost always automatically sent copies that the system purchased for all branches. (This is also how we ended up with multiple copies of popular books—James Comey's *A Higher Loyalty* and J. D. Vance's *Hillbilly Elegy*—that took up shelf space after interest and the lengthy hold lists had dwindled.)

I explained most of this to the students that day. And then I told them about my visit to the Riverside Public Library, and how I'd struggled to find books that featured characters that reflected the demographics of the city we lived in and of the students who were looking back at me as I spoke. Only a few of the students in the course were White—maybe two or three, at most. Hands shot up to ask what they could do about this and how it had happened. I encouraged them to visit the library and inquire about making ordering requests, as nearly all library systems have some sort of system for patron recommendations, and I wrote the e-mail address for someone to contact at the library on the whiteboard. A few students who were parents stayed after class to ask me for titles that included characters who reflected the experiences, and appearances, of them and their children. I saw another teaching moment when I explained that oftentimes these books were written about trauma, grief, or physical acceptance, not joy or everyday life experiences. Again I saw anger and hurt in their eyes. I went home and created several individualized book lists and sent them to students with resources for where they could borrow or purchase them at low cost if they weren't available at the library.

This was the first work I engaged in around libraries, post–library work, that I felt positive about. I was learning how to exist in the world as a former librarian and not a working one. Nine years of my life—most of my adulthood—had been focused on becoming and being a librarian, and I had wanted to abandon that knowledge and experience when I arrived in California, to be a student and a writer only. I had wanted a clean separation between the two, and I thought, if anything, the width of the country could probably achieve that. But the library and what I had seen and learned there showed up in my life constantly.

A few days after teaching the undergraduate students, I was in a Starbucks drive-through when I saw a middle-aged Black man sitting on the curb. He was wearing ripped and stained clothing, and the garbage bag next to him had a sleeping bag protruding from it. It was just before noon, and the Southern California heat was laser beaming; even with my air conditioning on, I could feel it through the windshield. A week earlier, I'd bought a breakfast sandwich and coffee for a different man sitting in the same spot with a sign that read HUNGRY. As each driver inched forward in line, that man had mimed for them to roll their window down. This man did not have a sign, and he was not making eye contact with anyone. He was slumped and defeated, perhaps hoping someone would offer him food or money, or maybe not hoping for anything at all. I went back to my apartment without offering him anything, not even a hello.

Millions of Americans do this every day—pass by people struggling to meet their basic needs and choose not to help. It is second nature at this point for many. Over the years, I've had lengthy conversations with friends, colleagues, and strangers about ways to engage with people, especially unhoused people, that will not take an unnecessary stab at their dignity. Make eye contact, respond when they address you. If you're going to offer money, it is not your business how they spend it. If you're going to offer food and they don't want it, that does not make them ungrateful or a junkie or any other story you assign to them with whatever evidence you think you have. Sometimes an interaction may not end well, just like any interaction with any person. Be aware of your surroundings. Keep phone numbers for local shelters and shuttle services and emergency mental health care advocates in your phone. Ask if they'd like you to call someone for them. Stop and check if someone is breathing if you see them unmoving in a way that does not look like sleep.

When I pulled away from the drive-through that day, I felt something beyond the familiar senses of not helping, of being complicit within a country that has failed to adequately create solutions to provide livable housing for all its citizens. I felt what I had been avoiding: the ways I had failed at being a librarian. The many unhoused patrons at Northwest One whom I had never been able to help secure housing. The mistakes I had made. The times I did not intervene or intervened in ways that were harmful to others.

There is, of course, no way to make it through a life without making mistakes. Not in our personal lives, not in our working lives, and not in any of our many relationships that fall under one of those two broad categories. However unintended harm might be, intentions mean very little if damage to individuals, or communities, is done. At my librarian baseline, I wanted to provide access to resources and accurate information to anyone who needed or wanted it. And I wanted anyone who entered any library where I worked to feel safe asking me. What was harder to face was that some of my actions, or inactions, twisted the fate of others. It didn't matter whether that occurred because of a conscious or unconscious possession of power—it mattered that it happened.

I did not sit with the full weight of any of this when I was working as a librarian. I did, however, look everywhere outside of myself to place the blame first—the difficult branch I had been assigned, the empathy fatigue I was experiencing, the good intentions I had. I could not create space for looking at what I had done wrong—the times I had been impatient or unkind, the times I had not considered cultural difference, the times I had monitored areas of the library at length from a surveillance camera because someone was new and unfamiliar, the ways I had potentially harmed my coworkers, the unending list of minor and major interpersonal transgressions—because the reckoning and the subsequent guilt felt awful.

But everything, absolutely all the library work, had also been data. Collectible information that could be assessed and analyzed, that inferences could be made from. Some might argue that information and data, numbers and charts and statistics, aren't concerned with what *feels* "good" or "bad" (or any number of things in between), but I disagree. All data is tied back to emotions—to some original question, concern, desire, hypothesis that can be traced back to the feelings of a researcher, or a scientist, or whoever formed a hypothesis, asked a question, became interested in measuring something, tried to solve a problem or cure a virus, and so forth.

When I reviewed circulation statistics as a school librarian to help determine what books to purchase, my question may have been as specific as "Which Dewey classification number is checked out the most?" If the answer was 398.2, the organizing code for fairy tales and fables, I could recall which curriculum units teachers had asked students to check out these books for, potentially driving up the checkout numbers. I could think of individual students or teachers who had asked for specific fables we did not have in the collection and assess whether I should order multiple copies. I looked at the data, but I also thought about the humans. I had a relationship to data because the data involved a body of people I knew. The numbers were not just numbers—they were conversations I had with children about the books they read and returned, conversations with staff members about which books had done well or been duds at story time, which changes to the curricula meant we needed more books around specific topics.

Similarly, at the public library I could see which books brought people the most excitement and joy and made them come the most alive when they spoke about them. I could see which books were checked out again and again and which were abandoned halfway through. I observed each week during story time when a song or familiar character made caregivers and children sing louder or yell with excited anticipation. I made programming and outreach decisions based on these emotions, this humanness, this data, as well.

All this information was collected through, and with, emotions involved, however much it seemed removed in the conclusion or subsequent action.

My core understanding as a trained librarian that information and data lead to verifiable conclusions and change is not something I had ever intellectually applied to mistakes. Mistakes had only ever been about feelings, and those feelings were generally ones that were hard to face. Shame, vulnerability, guilt, frustration, anger. Framing them on a cognitive level as *information*, not just emotions, changed my relationship to them.

What I was learning in the aftermath of Northwest One, what was so uncomfortable, is that of course data is not beyond our reaction to it. And yet, however much mistakes provide information to make better decisions, this only happens deeply when we pause and allow space for our relationship to them to grow beyond just our emotional ties to them. Not everyone is allotted that time.

The biggest mistake I made in the year after leaving the library was not reflecting on the information I had spent the previous nine years gathering. I wanted to compartmentalize it, to store it away into some neat internal file and label it "Library," to look back on it when time had passed and it didn't hurt so much. This was a fair coping mechanism for the short term, but not the long term.

From childhood to now, the library has been my most difficult—most demanding and present—teacher. When I moved to California, when I chose that second path, I tried to look away from the other one, and I could not. The lens I had developed at the library continued—even through all my exhaustion—to influence how I saw the world around me.

———————

The American public library is a case study for American society: what we value and uphold, what we resist and weave stories around, whom we give certain access to and whom we deny it. I finally became curious about what public libraries could teach us about American society, once I had physical and emotional distance from the space where I had observed it. I started to see the library not necessarily as a failing solution or a shoddy fix-all, but rather as *information* about American society and culture. I started to think about how the American public library might move forward differently, and then how it might be one great teacher in how we move forward as a country. I stopped permitting myself so much time to think about *me* and started to think about *we* again. This only happened because I had the time, space, health insurance, and money that I needed to comfortably and safely reflect. My physical and mental health were not as directly on the line in California, away from libraries.

I could dig into librarianship, and libraries, without so many of my own agonizing emotions attached.

Many care workers and people in helping professions never get this space and time. And the institutions they work within remain unchanged, or are much slower to change, precisely because workers are too overextended to fight for better circumstances. Much of this can be tied to living in a capitalistic society that values profit over people and productivity over rest and fosters the ease and relative safety of being complicit by emphasizing the risk of expressing concerns and unionizing, but the controls of capitalism certainly affect some demographics more than others. An example of this from my Rust Belt hometown is that when manufacturing jobs disappeared in Buffalo, the White, less educated working class was deeply impacted, and the despair many felt led to increased opioid use and suicides among this population. But Black workers who lost manufacturing jobs in these same cities were already at a disadvantage because of discriminatory housing and lending policies and were hit much harder. While parallels can always be made between impacted groups, it is important to note that people who are not White have been negatively affected more, and by more factors. Across all demographics, though, there is often no time, money, or energy to fight back and change the systems that create and uphold these working and living conditions. As my father often said to us growing up, the fact remains that you have to do what you have to do to keep a roof over your head and food on the table. When you are struggling to meet basic needs, there is little to no time to consider why and how your life circumstances might be different.

I had the luxury, the privilege, of that thinking time in California for the first time in my life. When I reflected on and considered my years in DC more fully, I saw the many ways that everyone in the shared space of the library was negatively impacted by the distractions of capitalism and all the many things like empathy fatigue, burnout, substance abuse, and mental health disorders that exist, in large part, because of capitalism's hold on our economy and society. It overwhelmed and angered and saddened me deeply, but I was determined to use the time ahead of me to tackle what I could, how I could, with the time I had.

10

LIBRARIES WILL (NOT) SAVE US

If you become interested in the health of the place where you are, whether that's cultural or biological or both, I have a warning: you will see more destruction than progress.

—Jenny Odell, *How to Do Nothing: Resisting the Attention Economy*

IN OCTOBER OF 2013, author Neil Gaiman published an edited version of a lecture he gave in 2012 in the *Guardian* with the title "Why Our Future Depends on Libraries, Reading and Daydreaming." It evoked familiar refrains of why libraries are so valuable as safe community spaces and repositories of information that give equal access to all citizens, noting that they provide "a haven from the world."[1]

Two days after the 2016 US presidential election, the *Los Angeles Times* ran a column titled "How to Weather the Trump Administration: Head to the Library." Penned by David Kipen, the former literature director of the National Endowment for the Arts, it read, in part: "Even now, in this riven country, after this whole entropically hideous year, most Americans still agree on at least one institution. Mercifully, it's the one that may just save us: the public library."[2]

In May of 2017, *Fortune* published an article titled "Librarians Will Save Us All" in which the author wrote how librarians have "nailed the safe space thing."[3]

In September of 2020, the *New York Times* published an opinion piece with the headline "How Libraries Can Save the 2020 Election." It noted that libraries are among our last trusted institutions and that expanding early voting at local branches may be the best hope for future trusted election outcomes.[4]

The president and chief executive of the New York Public Library, Anthony Marx, was cited in a September 2020 *New York Times* article as saying, "Given that the country is tearing itself apart, perhaps libraries can help to repair our civic fabric."[5]

In late March of 2020, the *Atlantic* published a story for part of their Our Towns series that began by stating that America's public libraries have "led the ranks of 'second responders.'"[6] Deborah Fallows, one half of the husband-and-wife team behind the series, had written a previous story for the publication in 2019 about how she'd first come to think of libraries as playing this role. Born and raised in DC, she described visiting a DC public library and speaking with librarians: "[Librarians] say that occasionally people are placed on 'sabbatical' from the libraries for infringements and are sometimes referred to public places where they can take showers. None have reported serious incidents to me, which suggests that respect is mutual."[7]

This one got to me the most. Where Fallows had written "sabbatical," DCPL workers would have said "barred." And then there was the issue of calling librarians "second responders."

The US Department of Homeland Security defines *first* responders as any individual who in the early stages of an incident is responsible for the protection and preservation of life, property, evidence, and the environment. A *second* responder, on the other hand, is a worker who supports the first responders during and after an event requiring first responders. Second responders are involved in the overall preparing, managing, and cleaning up of sites (like crime scenes and areas damaged by fire, storms, wind, floods, earthquakes, or other natural disasters).

To qualify as a first responder—a fireman, a police officer, a paramedic—certain amounts of training are required. First responders are formally, and then practically, trained for the diverse and unpredictable mental, emotional, physical, or manual labor that may be required of them. By the nature of their jobs, first responders know that they will be called to emergencies. The most commonly referred to first responders are people like firefighters and EMTs, but the Homeland Security Act of 2002 expanded the term to include people in emergency management, public health, clinical care, public works, and other skilled support personnel who provide immediate care during prevention, response, and recovery operations.

It is essentially second responders who pick up the pieces after the initial shattering. And though it's probably not the first profession to come to mind, librarians often play the role of both first and second responder in their work, not just second responder.

Imagine someone is overdosing in the library. A library worker calls a first responder—in this case, usually paramedics—to provide emergency medical attention. The library worker, as a second responder, is responsible for the aftercare. This can range from gathering statements from witnesses, consoling confused or concerned bystanders, and performing custodial duties, as a medical emergency often requires cleanup, including of biohazardous materials. If we consider a library that is stocked with Narcan kits and has librarians trained in how to administer it to persons overdosing, between calling emergency personnel and those responders' arrival, the librarian will have acted as a first responder by providing the initial, and often lifesaving, care. The librarian then also fulfills the role of second responder in the aftermath.

Another common crisis that occurs in library spaces is a patron suffering a psychotic episode. A librarian may press a panic button, or otherwise call for help, but again, they are responsible for managing the situation while additional help is on the way. The librarian may attempt to calm the patron and keep space between them and others in case they behave violently, and a librarian may also utilize de-escalation skills they have formally or informally been trained in. This work of being both first and second responder is often missing in conversations about the daily challenges facing librarians in the field.

The many and varied calls for libraries to "save" us often come on the cusp, or in the immediate aftermath, of national crises. The 2020 Fallows

Atlantic piece includes conjecture that libraries were positively acting and improvising in response to the coronavirus pandemic, noting that libraries would not understand the impact the pandemic had on them until later when "they'll be figuring out what the experience means to their future operations and their role in American communities."[8] This implication that libraries were stepping up in ways they never had before is true. But this has less to do with libraries never responding to crises before and more to do with the global impact of this specific crisis, the first global pandemic in the lifetime of American public libraries.

In 2005, the year of hurricanes Katrina and Rita, a Federal Emergency Management Agency (FEMA) representative in Cameron Parish, Louisiana, said plainly, "Libraries are not essential services." And yet all evidence pointed to the contrary. One survey found that in the months following the hurricanes half of all respondents and 40 percent of people interviewed used libraries in New Orleans for reasons including Internet access, information and technology assistance, mental escape, and refuge.[9] Participants also discussed how the destruction of libraries added to their sense of loss, and the eventual restoration of libraries gave them a sense of hope.[10] Similarly, after Hurricane Sandy, libraries all over the Eastern Seaboard distributed food and beverages, acted as distribution centers for emergency supplies, set up projectors to keep a newsfeed going during operating hours, and hosted additional children's programs while schools were closed. After Hurricane Maria in 2017, a public librarian from the town of Gurabo, Puerto Rico, told *American Libraries* magazine that "receiving access to information is a right of every person, and I am going to do everything I can to reopen this library."[11]

As part of the Stafford Act of 2010, FEMA now recognizes libraries among essential services, adding them to a category that includes police, fire protection/emergency services, medical care, education, and utilities. But this designation was made without a clear understanding of how libraries *should* support their communities, which has sometimes led to confusion in subsequent emergencies, including the COVID-19 pandemic.

Public libraries and library workers have stepped in during every major American crisis in recent history, not just the most recent and prevalent in our minds. Critics and culture writers certainly aren't the only ones banking on libraries' and librarians' abilities to compensate for our lack of sustainable social safety nets and infrastructure. Libraries and librarians are used to working in these capacities, in the unpredicted and unpredictable. They have regularly responded to crises without any established protocol for how to best do so, relying instead on their skills and intimate knowledge of their communities to anticipate needs, and reevaluate them, as time passes. And whereas emergency teams, government agencies, and first responders will eventually withdraw, libraries and librarians remain there in the community, helping to pick up the pieces and assist with related needs for years to come. In many cases, crises have caused library systems, libraries, and librarians to undergo a paradigm shift, with a revision of services and development of innovative ways to work more efficiently and effectively. All of this comes with immense labor and potential conflicts among librarians and library systems as all try to determine new best practices.

In addition to libraries' responses in the aftermath of natural disasters, there are countless other examples from our past of libraries stepping in to create provisional solutions.

During the height of the AIDS pandemic, the West Hollywood branch library in Los Angeles was specifically chosen as the site for a collection of resources about AIDS because it was felt that there would be less of a potential stigma for patrons entering a public library than going to an AIDS facility for information.[12] Other libraries in the area worked with AIDS activist groups, created ongoing displays, and distributed pamphlets and other informational material.

In New York City after the September 11 attack on the Twin Towers, branch and research libraries stayed open, an act that many considered a reassuring symbol to the community. Reading rooms were packed with people in search of not just information, but a sense of community, safety, and some slice of normalcy. In a January 2002 editorial in *American Libraries*, editor in chief Leonard Kniffel wrote that "knowing that an anti-Muslim backlash was inevitable, [the librarians] created programs to help the patrons of their libraries understand the teachings of Islam, the history of American policy related to the conflict we now find ourselves in, and what it means to be a Muslim in America."[13]

In November 2014, when the grand jury failed to indict the policeman responsible for the shooting of Michael Brown in Ferguson, Missouri, the Ferguson Municipal Public Library kept open throughout the crisis, partnering with teachers and community agencies to provide education, information, and emotional support to the community. One librarian noted that "the most important thing during the unrest was that all the library staff stayed neutral towards the whole situation. All patrons, whether they were protestors or against protesting, were welcome to visit the library, use its resources and facilities, and request help and assistance from the staff, who tried to avoid talking about politics." Another staff member noted that "when some patrons felt disenfranchised with the community and the government, we were trying to be the one government entity that people could trust at that time."[14] It was likely that both of these librarians were also living within these same communities and struggling to find the best ways to respond. In their daily work librarians make individual choices and have their own approaches, sometimes with minimal oversight and guidance, especially in the midst of crises. At a minimum, library and librarian responses to civil unrest have helped ease some of the trauma, tension, and fear within communities simply by remaining open to the public and providing a familiar sense of normalcy. As another FMPL library employee put it, "If you need to make a photocopy, you can still go to your library even though it seems like the whole world is falling apart around you, you can still do the thing that you need to do to make it through your day."[15]

In response to the rising numbers of overdoses in libraries across the country, library workers in rural, urban, and suburban settings have been trained to administer Narcan to help reverse overdoses. Many libraries, from the Barrington Public Library in Rhode Island to the Everett Public Library in Washington State to the New Orleans Public Library in Louisiana, have offered naloxone training to the public as well.

Salt Lake County Library in Utah distributed naloxone and held a community education campaign on opioid misuse, partnering with a local ad agency to implement a marketing campaign at the library titled "Use Only As Directed." The campaign depicted the magnitude of opioid prescriptions filled each day in Utah by hanging seven thousand pill bottles from the library ceiling.

Twinsburg Public Library in Twinsburg, Ohio, hosted an unused medication disposal by distributing Deterra bags that people could use in the privacy of their own homes.

In Blount County, Tennessee, there was a multiyear effort between the public library and a Recovery Court to design and deliver the Life Skills Curriculum geared toward helping people recovering from addiction with career development, nutrition, social and physical health, and so on. The Kalamazoo Public Library in Kalamazoo, Michigan, added sharps containers to its restrooms.[16]

Most of these libraries financed their responses through their own operating budgets and staff time or had the activity paid for or provided in kind by community partners. This list continues and includes hundreds of libraries all over the country.

Libraries and librarians have responded with typical resourcefulness and flexibility during the COVID-19 pandemic. In San Francisco, libraries became emergency childcare centers for frontline workers. In Toledo, Ohio, the public library system offered their vehicles to organizations delivering food supplies. In Anchorage, Alaska, the city's emergency operations system moved into a library for more space and better Wi-Fi connectivity.[17] The San José Public Library in California used additional coronavirus relief funds to build out Wi-Fi at branches and distribute eleven thousand free hot spots to the community as work, school, and life switched online.[18] And many libraries expanded general services like online renewal policies and reference services, increased online programming, and added curbside and contactless library hold pickups.

When there are hurricanes, tornadoes, mass shootings, election fraud, and other incidents that cause collective distress, librarians have adjusted their hours, services, resources, and outreach to meet the needs of their community members. Librarians are clearly key contributors to community resiliency. It is easy to see how everyone from newspaper columnists to everyday citizens believes in the possibility of libraries saving us, even as what we need saving from constantly changes and grows.

And yet, despite all this prophesying and placement of hope in public libraries, despite all the ever-evolving work librarians complete, their significance—including conversations surrounding their funding—remains in question and under debate. There is a similarly long list of recent articles to the ones I opened this chapter with that question the future of public libraries and if they have one at all. Will libraries as public spaces remain relevant given our increasing reliance on digital data? If so, can librarians sustain the evolving changes of what it means to be a librarian? Will libraries withstand the move to privatize so many of our public institutions? Do people even still go to libraries?

The answer to all these questions is yes. Has been yes, will continue to be yes.

Every few months, a friend sends me some version of a notion they've seen in a tweet or other social media post: if public libraries were invented today, our society and government would never let them happen. My response is this: I don't think we would be here, period, without public libraries. Without centuries of information that has been protected, preserved, disseminated, cataloged, or otherwise organized and shared to help guide us through every pivotal moment in modern history. And not just pivotal moments, but mundane ones, joyful ones, sorrowful ones. There is a reason that libraries have existed in some form as far back as the seventh century BC and that philosophers, historians, monarchs, peasants, and any other category of human beings we have created have turned to them for guidance, entertainment, and a sense of place in the world. They provide answers. They preserve history. They mark our humanness, our present, our past, our future.

One of the most prevalent oppositions to the necessity of libraries that people voice is the development and advancement of technology. In these instances, I would point people to link rot. Link rot is the tendency of Internet links over time to no longer direct to their originally intended content or to break altogether. We might consider the Internet as one giant library that is managed by no one person, or groups of persons, in particular. As Google itself puts it on its page titled "How Search Organizes Information": "The web is like an ever-growing library with billions of books and no central filing system."[19] While this is cited and celebrated as one of its greatest qualities—the overall freedom of speech and expression, of democracy and grassroots perseverance, that the Internet allows for and fosters—it has also altered how we preserve our histories. Never have our recorded histories been more susceptible to erasure, compromise, and deletion in ways that physical libraries are not because they are run by living, breathing librarians who maintain them. As Jonathan Zittrain, a professor of law and computer science at Harvard, writes: "Imagine if libraries didn't exist and there was only a 'sharing economy' for physical books: People could register what books they happened to have at home, and then others who wanted them could visit and peruse them. It's no surprise that such a system could fall out of date, with books no longer where they were advertised to be—especially if someone reported a book being in someone else's home in 2015, and then an interested reader saw that 2015 report in 2021 and tried to visit the original home mentioned as holding it. That's what we have right now on the web."[20] Zittrain has extensively examined and consciously critiqued the Internet for years now and has identified many faults to how we organize and protect the integrity of online information. At perhaps his most cautious he warns about the inevitable susceptibility of e-books and similar forms of publishing to become new areas for censorship, noting that suing writers for defamation has become far easier. He uses the example of rereading a favorite passage of a favorite book that has undergone a slight tweak on a Kindle, how the reader experiences "only a nagging feeling that it isn't quite how one remembers it." Such examples already exist, with authors requesting that publishers delete passages that others found offensive from the digital—and most easy to change—version of their books, in one case in response to demands made on Twitter.[21]

These questions of how libraries will remain relevant in the digital age turn up again and again, often with conjecture about how e-books might replace physical books—or how they already have—how the Internet has replaced librarians, how a physical space like a library is no longer needed the same way it used to be. These questions arise from a lack of understanding of the faultiness of the Internet and also the many roles libraries play in society outside of being repositories of books.

I do not foresee any type of future where librarians are not relevant, necessary, and cherished. To the patrons who use them, to the writers and lawyers and activists and politicians who thank them in speeches and tweets and interviews, to the caregiver who takes their child to story time, to the people who stop to sip the cool library water fountain like a sacred routine, to the journalists who after every crisis evoke their society-saving abilities. To most Americans. And yes, libraries will continue to be physical structures that house books and provide free access to the Internet and answers and so much more. Absolutely.

The larger question, the one I am most interested in now, is whether libraries and librarians *should* continue to carry so much of the weight of emergencies and crises.

———————

As a means of investigating this, I created and shared a survey on social media in May 2020 and asked librarians, past and current, to fill it out.

Some of the questions I included were:

- Do you think your MLS program properly prepared you for the actuality of library work?
- Have you ever feared for your physical safety at work?
- Have you ever experienced (or are you currently experiencing) empathy fatigue from your work?
- Do you feel comfortable speaking to your managers and/or administrators about concerns for yourself and/or library users?
- Does your library have a panic/duress button?
- Does your library system and/or library branch employ library police officers or security guards?

I received seventy responses from public librarians in twenty-eight states and the District of Columbia. The librarians ranged in professional experience from one year to more than twenty-five years working in public libraries. The data I gathered confirmed many of my own experiences: Fifty-eight out of seventy librarians replied "yes" to feeling unsafe at work, and fifty-seven replied "yes" to being verbally assaulted at work (seven replied "yes" to being physically assaulted as well). Fifty-two of seventy librarians responded "yes" to experiencing, or having experienced, empathy fatigue at work, with an additional eight responding "I'm not sure."

I was most moved by responses I received to questions that did not have multiple-choice options, but rather, blank spaces to respond. One of those questions was the final one on the survey: "Is there anything else you want to tell me about yourself or your experiences?"

Thirty-nine out of the seventy librarians responded:

"I feel like my passion has been stolen from me."

"I'm really young and I'm finding that this quickly might wear me out."

"I have witnessed library security handcuff a child in an argument that began because the library gave security permission to police noise in the library. I've listened to a manager say 'these kids will be dead in a few years anyway' in an inner-city library. I've been told the 'safe place' sticker on the door is cosmetic. I've heard a security guard theorize a situation in which he would shoot the children at the library. I've been reprimanded for prioritizing children and teens over security. I don't work for that system anymore."

"There are times, like now, where no matter how much I love my job and am passionate about it, I really just feel like I need to walk away, because it's too consuming of my mental and emotional bandwidth. I'm not sure I will, but it's the planning for an alternate future for myself that keeps me going sometimes. I had a health scare last year, and my library was so supportive, I felt like I could never leave, because I could never have it that good anywhere else. But I'm reevaluating every day. We'll see."

"Things have a different feel, and though we have some wonderful families and I have wonderful coworkers, I am counting down the days until retirement. In the last year, I have been called so many names, have cleaned up so much poop—thank God I was on vacation during the Poop-ocalypse—have asked so many Teens to 'leave room for the Holy Ghost,' and have had to tell a 20-something that most people don't cut their toenails in public places. I am SO ready for the next adventure!"

"I've found myself becoming more cynical and jaded as a librarian. I also find it disheartening that so few people outside the library realize just how much library workers put up with. It's like a dirty secret people are fearful to talk about. We have to put on this happy, cheery facade of 'everything is fine' for fear of what? Losing public funding? I can't even decompress and share the horrors of my experience with nonlibrary people because the attitude is 'you read books all day, how bad can it be.'"

Librarian after librarian, all across the country, also echoed the lack of support they felt, specifically from administrators:

"I love libraries and I wish mine did a better job, but I'll keep working hard and climbing the ladder until I am making the decisions."

"My manager is often undercut by her deputies, who are in turn blindsided by the board of supervisors, admin, and/or the county librarian."

The set of survey responses that rattled me most came in response to the question "If you are no longer a librarian/library worker, why did you leave?" As I was reading through the gathered answers on an Excel spreadsheet, I spotted two of the same responses and assumed someone had submitted their answers twice. When I looked closer, I realized that two librarians from entirely different systems—one in western New York, the other in rural Illinois—had answered the question with the exact same words, in the exact same order:

"I felt unsupported, I felt burned out, I felt unsafe."

The librarian in Illinois had added, "Low pay looking to leave" to the end of the statements, and the librarian in New York finished with, "I'm actively trying to change careers due to [these] factors." The New York librarian had marked working as a librarian for five to ten years and the one in Illinois for fifteen to twenty. A librarian who had been working for more than twenty-five years in Arizona responded to the same question with, "I was too angry to function anymore." There were similar responses from the other five responding librarians who had left the field. I tried, as ever, to collect the data of it all, and I absolutely saw and felt emotions. One librarian left a final comment that I "seem worried," and I was. I was also angry. Angry in a way I hadn't felt since leaving Northwest One.

Many of the survey responses spoke directly to the empathy fatigue, exhaustion, and lack of support that I knew intimately. The feelings of fear, burnout, and helplessness were shared, mutual, systemic—by librarians all over the country. Some remained more optimistic or devoted— thirty-seven librarians responded that yes, they would remain a librarian until retirement—but the majority of them reported feeling burnout and exhaustion, defeat and low morale. I sent the survey out during the early months of the COVID-19 pandemic, and even though I was nearing two full years outside the profession, I was angry at the prospect of public libraries reopening during a pandemic before it was safe, without proper supplies and support. I was angry that librarians were being asked to put their bodies on the line in more and more ways. Angry that my writing about libraries had been called "dark" and "too pessimistic" by editors and publishers.

When the most acute of my anger passed, I felt deep and sinking grief. I had not been alone all those years in libraries.

To better understand how and why libraries respond to crises, it is important to understand that there is something of a rift among librarians and that they can, for the most part, be broken into two groups. Group one believes library professionals sign up to be in deep service to their community and understand that they may be called on as second, and sometimes first, responders. Group two believes they signed up to be information professionals and protectors of freedom of speech, not emergency responders. There is plenty of crossover between these two philosophies, but every librarian I know or have interviewed leans one way more than the other. Emergencies of any kind are often the way to see where a person sits on this spectrum.

When faced with having to approach a patron who has been locked in a single-use bathroom, a librarian from group two might adopt the attitude that they "did not go to library school for this," while a librarian from group one would consider this monitoring a part of the job, even if they find it unpleasant. The group one librarian likely considers more carefully that this person maybe hadn't had access to clean water in weeks and was trying to bathe, or perhaps was unconscious and needed medical care. They might chastise a group two librarian, saying, "You knew when you signed up for this that you would have to deal with the public." The group two librarian might reply, "This was not what I was trained to do in school, and it is nowhere in my job duties as assigned."

In a more serious emergency, like a violent patron in the library space, a group two librarian might say, "I became a librarian to bring literature and information to the community, not to put my life at risk," whereas a librarian who leans more into group one would say, "These people are in our community, and we serve our community. Do your job."

Neither librarian is wrong—not by the standards that have been set by MLS programs all over the country, not by the American Library Association, and certainly not by any collective societal understanding about who and what libraries are and are not responsible for. Public libraries, as institutions made up of a body of librarians, usually walk some collective line near the middle of these two groups.

In my work as a librarian, I leaned toward being a group one librarian. I had an understanding that the role of librarian was first and foremost a public-facing one in service to the community. I knew that part of the job was that I would sometimes be called on to take on roles outside of the narrow scope many librarians initially believe they are signing up for. But I was also sometimes uncomfortable with just how much was required of me, and this feeling only grew the longer I worked as a librarian. Only now do I understand that I did not want to fulfill *either* of these roles, in large part because I did not feel equipped—either professionally or personally—to be what and who I needed to be. I did not, it turned out in the end, want to be a librarian.

I am not alone in these feelings or in leaving the profession after this realization, but many librarians do stay and try to change the scope of library services to both better serve their patrons and maintain their own mental and physical health and safety.

With that said, there is a largely unexamined history of librarians who have not been able to protect those things.

———————

On August 10, 1993, the *Los Angeles Times* published an article that began: "When the Los Angeles Central Library reopens this fall, seven years after an arsonist set it on fire, it will have all the accouterments of a modern library—including 100 surveillance cameras, motion detectors and access-control doors."[22] The fire mentioned is the one Susan Orlean writes about in *The Library Book*. The title of the piece is long, but it speaks volumes about a shift that was happening in libraries during the 1990s: "No Longer a Refuge for Readers: Libraries are Trying Off-Duty Police, Security Cameras to Counter Rising Crime. The Numbers of Street People Seeking Shelter Have Prompted Use of Such Extreme Measures as Odor Monitors." The piece outlines some examples of these measures: libraries in Miami hired off-duty police officers; a Chula Vista, California, library was coated with an "anti-graffiti melt" and a barricade of the thorny bougainvillea, and colleagues of two Sacramento librarians who were murdered by a patron demanded that panic buttons be installed behind their desks.

The 1993 murders in Sacramento were committed at the downtown branch of the library system by a thirty-eight-year-old man named Barrett L. Street. Street was unhoused and a regular library visitor with whom staff were familiar. On April 19, seemingly at random, Street went to the third floor of the branch and gunned down two employees at their workstations. He then ran to the roof of the library, where he was surrounded by police. As officers tried to talk to him, he began mumbling about how his wife hadn't been treated properly, though it was not clear if he meant at the library or somewhere else. Street refused to drop his gun, pointed it at officers, and was killed in a fusillade of twenty-five bullets. His body toppled from the roof to the street. When officers located his gun, it was empty.[23]

When I searched "Sacramento library murder" to learn more, the top results were all more recent news stories about the murder of another Sacramento librarian. Amber Clark was shot in the head and killed by Ronald Seay on December 11, 2018, as she sat in her car in the North Natomas library parking lot where she was the branch supervisor. Seay had been ordered to not trespass at the library after an incident in October when he had become aggressive toward staff and other patrons.

In the aftermath of Clark's murder, it was discovered that Seay had a documented history of violent threats and behavior toward librarians in both Ferguson and Brentwood, Missouri. Employees in Missouri had called 911 after Seay refused to leave a branch, and he told responding police, "I don't care. I'm coming back." Seay never appeared for his

Missouri court date, and somewhere in the five months before murdering Clark, he made his way to California. Two weeks before her murder, Amber had told her husband, Kelly Clark, who is also a librarian, that she was worried about being assaulted or shot at work.[24]

Incidents like these are not uncommon, especially in recent years:

On August 28, 2017, two librarians were murdered and four others were injured by a teenager in a Clovis, New Mexico, public library.[25]

On February 24, 2018, a man diagnosed with schizophrenia stabbed another library customer to death at a Winchester, Massachusetts, library.[26]

On January 20, 2019, the director of the Fort Myers Beach, Florida, library was stabbed to death by a patron.[27]

At a Spring Valley, New York, public library branch on February 19, 2020, a patron stabbed and killed library security guard Sandra Wilson.

This list continues.

In an article Kelly Clark published in *American Libraries* magazine after his wife's death titled *Keep Library Workers Safe*, he wrote, "In the wake of Amber's murder, I have come to seriously reassess my own role as a public library employee."[28] The comments section in response to the heartbreaking piece is full of library workers sharing their own stories of violence, both witnessed and experienced, in the library. Many people wrote about their managers, administrators, and library systems not doing more to protect their employees and patrons. One commenter responded that he was surprised the horrific incident had not sparked more of a conversation within the profession, and Clark replied at length that he was "acutely aware that speaking up might have the effect of rendering me *persona non grata*. However, that is a risk I am willing to take in light of the most emotionally challenging life experience I have ever faced."

The culture within the library and information science (LIS) profession often prevents real concerns from being heard, at least publicly, and this is often a culture established and upheld by administrators and other decision-making officials. Clark noted that the inherent problems public libraries face cannot be denied, and that denying them is a "dereliction of duty."

I felt for, and with, Kelly Clark and many of the commenters.

In 2017 librarian Katie McLain wrote a piece for the literary website Book Riot addressing what she referred to as the psychological toll of security threats after the library shooting in Clovis, New Mexico. I again saw familiar experiences in her writing: how she'd regularly call 911, how patrons screamed insults and racial slurs in her face, how men followed her into the shelving area and made increasingly uncomfortable comments about her appearance. McLain pointed to inadequate training and procedure, describing how in her first few years at the library she would run what-if scenarios in her head. "It's one thing to be prepared, and it's another thing to have these scenarios running through your head on a constant loop. . . . I wasn't trained on what our procedures were, and so I had to train and prepare myself every day just to get through a two-hour shift at the desk."[29] McLain also wrote about reaching out to her manager about the need for organization-wide discussions for how to handle potential issues and incidents. The many urgent, looming, and constant concerns for physical safety are in addition to the standard demands of library work like manning the circulation desk, reshelving, processing holds, conducting programming, and performing other daily tasks to make the library function. These were things I learned to do in my MLS program, as do all librarians. What I had not learned in my MLS program was crisis intervention or de-escalation skills. Any knowledge or resources I had came from my own research and lived experiences.

During my tenure, the DC Public Library had not required or provided any safety, de-escalation, or similar training, though a representative from DCPL reached out to one publication I gave an interview to in 2018 to claim that two trainings on helping vulnerable populations had been offered during my time with the system. I had never heard about either of them and confirmed with former coworkers that they did not know of any trainings during my time at the branch either. When I published an op-ed in the *Los Angeles Times* in April 2019 about my work at Northwest One, the editors gave it the title "Working as a Librarian Gave Me Post-Traumatic Stress Disorder Symptoms." I received backlash from some readers on the audacity of "claiming" PTSD—it was, one person commented, an insult to people who *actually* suffered from PTSD. I wrote the op-ed in response to viewing the 2018 Emilio Estevez film *The Public*, in which unhoused patrons who are unable to face another night in the subzero Cincinnati winter refuse to leave the public library and "occupy" it. It was the first time I had seen the job of public librarian accurately reflected on a big screen, and my overall hope in writing the piece was to draw attention to the realities of the many roles libraries and librarians are called on to play, many of which were seen in the film. After the piece was published, someone from DCPL again contacted the publication to deny parts of what I had written. I wished only to draw attention to a more complete story around libraries than the all too familiar one that has been perpetuated for hundreds of years.

In my first year after leaving Northwest One, I had not yet processed the experience, or my own errors within it, and sometimes spoke or wrote in ways that I regret. Some of this came out of a sense of urgency to get a more robust and truthful narrative around library work out there as powerfully and quickly as possible, but my own ignorance, prejudices, and anger were present as well. I will always, on some level, wish I had taken that first year to privately and silently reflect and learn. My desire to speak about my experiences came from a place of wanting to change the face of a discussion that all too often was untrue, incomplete, or dominated by voices who made decisions physically, and emotionally, away from the field.

If anything could lead to the downfall of public libraries, it would be a resistance to reckoning with their truths. Continuing to adopt personal or institutional attitudes against discussions of safety concerns in the library will do nothing to improve libraries for the communities they serve or for the librarians who work within them. Continuing to shut down productive conversations about resource inequity by saying that certain libraries or library systems are "unique" or "outliers" is completely, and verifiably, incorrect. There is abundant evidence against this argument.

It is entirely impossible for the singular institution of the public library to "save" us. This notion is rooted not just in incomplete information, but in a willful ignorance. The information—the voices—are out there, though, pleading to tell a different story.

From the perspective of someone who spent almost a decade in the field of librarianship, I am not disinterested in exploring information that is contrary to my own previously held beliefs or the beliefs most commonly accepted by others. I saw every day how pushing against accepted stories and norms, or having my own held beliefs pushed against, made my understanding of the world more holistic and nuanced. This has only ever benefited my abilities to show up in the world, especially when it has felt most difficult to. More globally, the refusal of institutions to look at the history, the roots, the *core* of so much happening in our country and the devastating impacts of embracing false narratives lead us back to the same negative ramifications. The same fragmented conversations, the same false conclusions, the same stagnation, again and again.

Where I remain optimistic is that libraries and librarians can help in significant ways here as models. Anyone can learn to think a little bit more like a librarian when it comes to not just research and information assessment, but also empathy and community care. Anyone can participate in this reckoning and think critically, and imaginatively, about how we might move forward.

11

MULTIPHRENIA

It is easier to tell a story of how people wound one
another than of what binds them together.

—Anne Carson, *Plainwater: Essays and Poetry*

WITH THE RISE OF WIDESPREAD DISINFORMATION during the 2016 US
presidential election and in the aftermath of Donald Trump's win, questions came to the circulation desk more often. On any given day, at least
one person would walk up, mention something Trump had said, tweeted,
or done the day or week before, and ask, "Can you look up if that's true?"
The interest around Hillary Clinton's e-mails was especially prevalent
in the winter of 2018, and I fielded many questions about them. When
there was time, I'd start these conversations by turning the computer
screen toward the patron to show them an article about how an FBI
investigation concluded that no reasonable prosecutor would bring a
criminal case against Clinton. Depending on patrons' political leanings,
this might branch into conjecture or conspiracy theories they had heard
elsewhere. Depending on how firmly patrons believed in their own established thoughts, unpacking an answer, or answers, sometimes took much
longer than I had time for. Many times I had to excuse myself from the
conversation or wrap it up to move on to helping someone else, but I
tried to leave patrons with a journalist's name or a book recommenda-
tion—something to guide them forward.

Oftentimes, the patrons I met at the desk simply craved connection and conversation. Every morning we put the day's issue of the *Washington Post* on the circ desk, and every day the first patron would come to collect it, sometimes holding up the front-page headline and saying, "Did you see this?" I'd look back at words I'd already seen blasted on my Twitter feed first thing that morning and say, "I did. I did." There was a mutual understanding that, by the nature of the library space and my position as a librarian, I would, to the best of my abilities, not display my own biases or voice judgments of the patrons' biases. I knew—or rather, I came to learn—that people were mostly trying to acknowledge the daily chaos with someone else. I understood because I craved the exact same thing.

There was an internal switch I had to turn off at the circulation desk that remained on in personal conversations. Had a close friend asked some of the questions I received ("Can you pull up the stuff in Hillary's emails where she's trying to sell kids?" "Is abortion murder?"), I would have automatically responded, "Are you serious?" But a patron's inquiry came without personal, familial knowledge. I didn't know patrons outside the library, and they did not always openly share their opinions or political affiliations. I couldn't understand their biases. And as a librarian, I didn't need to. They had a question, they entrusted it to me, and I did my best to answer it. It was not my job to judge people's questions or find moral fault with them, or to investigate their motive; it was my job to help them find answers.

I'll reiterate here that these kinds of interactions were possible in large part because of the library space and general expectations people have when they enter it. Librarians, by the nature of their job, are usually not openly judgmental or combatant. This is not to imply that librarians are neutral in their personal lives or even in their professional lives. They are not. But most librarians fight against censorship in all mediums, not just by providing information, but by protecting and upholding it, and by adopting similar approaches as I did—receive a question, find an answer, show your process. Librarians do all of this without any exact protocol for how to respond, instead relying on trained and developed research skills as well as their knowledge of their community to anticipate needs and reevaluate them as time passes and new questions arise.

Some of my deepest gratitude to the librarian profession comes from this practiced ability to remove myself as much as possible while seeking information. It was not necessarily easy or comfortable, but it was essential to the work. Disseminating information without passing judgment or attempting to influence the information with your own values is not easy or always possible though. I had (and still have) my own preferences for what resources I use for news and research, but this was something I was aware of at the desk, even on my worst and most depleted days. I worked with my computer screen turned toward the patrons as often as possible, making a point of clicking on author bios and scrolling down to any citations and footnotes when accessing articles or journals. The patron usually felt either impatient or curious about this.

"Why are you reading about the writer?"

"Oh, I always like to have an idea of whose work I'm reading."

"Why?"

"I like to see if they write around this topic often or if they've written anything more recent about it. I also like having a basic idea of who is writing—what their expertise and interests are."

Patrons who did not want to follow these bread crumbs with me said so, and certainly I did not always have time for this kind of guided inquiry. But sometimes I did, and we would discover something together: That the author had a more recent piece, with more developed or updated information on the topic, than the one I'd pulled up. Or that this was a freelance writer writing for a publication for the first time, so I'd jot down the writer's website on a slip of paper, so the patron could use a computer in the computer lab to see what else the writer was working on. My goal was to provide context and data to these more complicated questions, offering a response that went beyond a yes or no answer. I wasn't trying to prove or disprove anything (though sometimes that happened in our shared process); I was modeling how to access and then assess information, and in the most ideal outcome, I was helping patrons see how they could make their own conclusions or ask new questions. That research could be fascinating, especially if you slowed down for a moment. It was not always easy to turn down my emotions and reactions when someone asked something that I found offensive or incorrect or even foolish, but it became second nature at the circulation desk eventually to breathe through these moments and focus on the information-seeking process.

Like many other people born in the 1980s I took in information differently as a child. My family didn't get our first home computer until I was in middle school, and even then, we only had access to e-mail through a free e-mail service, Juno, which we downloaded off CDs placed in the Sunday newspaper inserts. We didn't get full Internet access until a couple of years later, and it was dial-up Internet until I was well into high school. I went into chat rooms on AOL at friends' houses, and we practiced adopting ages, genders, and interests different from our own. We pretended to be people we weren't and people we wanted to be, and then we went back to life away from the screen. I completed research for a final research project my senior year of high school mostly in the school's library on a huge manila-colored desktop computer using PowerPoint, Ask Jeeves, and Yahoo. I used Diaryland and then LiveJournal to begin logging my thoughts on our family's home computer—my earliest bits of writing outside of a notebook and available on the Internet—and I didn't get my first cell phone until my seventeenth birthday. When I did get one, it only had call and text-message capabilities, and I did not pay the extra monthly amount to send and receive text messages until two years later. A phone with much else would have been almost unfathomable to me back then. I didn't own a laptop until my second year of undergraduate, and I mostly used it for writing papers.

In addition to a mostly device-free childhood and teen years, for as long as I can remember, my parents have kept a collection of books on the two shelves underneath the television in their living room. In elementary and middle school, it was at eye level from where I preferred to lie on the floor to watch cartoons and episodes of *Little House on the Prairie*. To this day, the bottom shelf holds the complete *Funk and Wagnalls New Encyclopedia*, and the shelf above it has a standard dictionary, a medical dictionary, a thesaurus, and volumes 1 and 2 of the Doubleday *Complete Works of Shakespeare*. The Shakespeare volumes were ones that my mother had saved for and bought from a high school book club, and the encyclopedias were purchased when I was young, one volume at a time, from the grocery store. Every time my mother spent a certain dollar amount on groceries, she could purchase a new book of the encyclopedia at a bargain price until we finally owned the complete collection.

When I had a question as a child, I went to these shelves to find an answer. I remember this way of gathering information as joyful and satisfying. I would search the twelve gold-and-brown encyclopedia spines and find the one I needed, flipping through the pages until I located the word or concept I was looking for. It was rewarding—not unlike a treasure hunt in my young mind—to land in the right place. My understanding and love of information seeking was rooted here—in the books my mother had saved for and cleverly planted kid level. I sometimes spent hours reading pages from the thesaurus and dictionary for fun, forgetting the television altogether. I can't imagine how different I would be now if I had not been free and encouraged to seek answers in these ways, without external judgment or data tracking.

This level of curiosity has changed in the information age. In the early days of the widespread Internet, we logged off and walked away from computers when we finished whatever we were doing on them. We carried on with our off-line lives. The Internet was in one part of our home, usually on one computer, and we went to it like a destination—the same way we'd run out to a particular store for groceries or mail something at the post office.

Many people talk about "going down the rabbit hole" of Wikipedia or Reddit, where there are billions of holes that go much deeper now than twenty and thirty years ago, and where information is often incorrect, incomplete, or unverifiable. While this certainly requires a level of interest and curiosity to sift through and disseminate, it is different from the slowed-down research of my youth. With the Internet always available in the devices glued to our hands, it's not just our curiosity that has become muted (if not obliterated altogether), but also our time. Academics, journalists, and other writers often refer to this overload of information as *context collapse*, something Jenny Odell brilliantly unpacks in chapter 6 of her book *How to Do Nothing: Resisting the Attention Economy*. The term might most easily be understood as referring to the infinite possible online audiences available to us now through social media and other forms of technology as opposed to the limited groups a person normally interacts with in face-to-face conversations. There are those who limit or abstain entirely from social media use, but those people have become fewer and fewer in the last ten years especially.

In December 2009, 26 percent of American adults reported using at least one social media site, and by February of 2021, 72 percent did.[1] People in marginalized groups, including those experiencing houselessness, have social media accounts as well. Multiple studies show that more than 80 percent of unhoused youth have a Facebook profile and approximately 60 percent have smartphones. At the library, unhoused patrons often borrowed chargers to charge their phones and logged on to social media sites in the computer lab.[2]

In a 2009 speech to the plebe class at the United States Military Academy at West Point, author and literary critic William Deresiewicz cautioned the graduates about their constant exposure to social and news media: "You are continuously bombarding yourself with a stream of other people's thoughts. You are marinating yourself in the conventional wisdom. In other people's reality: for others, not for yourself. You are creating a cacophony in which it is impossible to hear your own voice, whether it's yourself you're thinking about or anything else."[3] The term *conventional wisdom* that he references was first coined by John Kenneth Galbraith in his 1958 book *The Affluent Society* and refers to unoriginal, predictable, and broadly accepted ideas that provide a certain kind of convenience and ease, with Galbraith writing that "the enemy of conventional wisdom is not ideas, but the march of events."[4] In ideal circumstances, the cacophony Deresiewicz warns against disappears at a library's circulation desk when a question becomes a shared, human-to-human exploration. Conventional wisdom, as Galbraith means it, becomes narrower, and easier to sort out our thoughts within. A certain marching forward into analyzing and understanding begins.

My years of experience fielding young people's questions in school libraries had in many ways uniquely prepared me to better understand the thoughts and emotions behind adults' questions as well. For over five years, I had watched in real time as my elementary-aged students discovered new information and tried to process it, information that often presented them, and me, with a long list of follow-up questions. Some of my favorite parts of being a school librarian were witnessing these moments of inquiry and seeing the excitement that came from finding one answer and then seeking another.

When I was still a school librarian, I supported a piece of a second-grade curriculum focused on teaching students how to use an encyclopedia. The school district had online access to *Britannica*, but I always started with the set of physical encyclopedias stored on shelves in the back of the teaching classroom. My two second grade classes would moan and groan, already aware that they could be learning how to do this much more quickly on a computer, until I let them know they could choose any word they wanted (ANY word? *Any* word).

They wrote their chosen word in the center of construction-paper kite shapes I'd cut out in different colors and piled into stacks. On each of the kite's four points they'd write down a fact they learned about from their research, and on the kite's tail, they'd add three construction-paper bows to be labeled with the page number they found it on and the word that came just before and just after it in the encyclopedia. My hope was that they would become curious about those words too, and they often did. Whenever I did this activity, students would ask if they could do another one and then another. The computers sat on their charging cart, and no one asked about opening them. Our library walls became decorated with colorful kites and bows, and students from all grade levels stopped to look at them, asking how and why they had been made. I also taught students how to use the online encyclopedia, but nearly all of them preferred the print version.

I saw a similar curiosity come to life with adults in conversations at the circulation desk—these visible aha moments at finding an answer, or the delight of sharing their perspective with someone else, knowing I would engage with them. In all the daily chaos that Northwest One often brought, these moments still happened every day, too. I'll repeat here that these kinds of interactions were possible in large part because there is less fear associated with speaking to a librarian than to a stranger. Library work offers a critical person: one who can help separate what has happened from how an individual *feels* about it. With a neutral stance, they can provide information to help the patron decide how they actually feel, not just what an algorithm or podcast or article or institution or individual wants to sway them to feel. In a time when people gravitate toward binary thinking—either/or, good/bad—because it feels like a more certain and safe place to land than the gray area of both/and, the way librarians think, learn, and teach remains essential. Librarians can model and teach these skills and still not reach their patrons though. And as I outline in the previous chapter, it is not possible for librarians to "save" us in these times of political and social unrest, context collapse, and disinformation. But I remain resolute that librarians and library work have been, and remain, some of our greatest teachers when it comes to information.

I gave an assignment* to students in the English composition class I taught at UC Riverside in which I asked them to adopt a "parlor conversation" lens around Twitter in order to give context to a larger essay assignment where they adopt an "academic conversation" lens. I introduced the idea of parlor conversation by having them read an excerpt from American literary theorist Kenneth Burke's *The Philosophy of Literary Form*:

> Imagine that you enter a parlor. You come late. When you arrive, others have long preceded you, and they are engaged in a heated discussion, a discussion too heated for them to pause and tell you exactly what it is about. In fact, the discussion had already begun long before any of them got there, so that no one present is qualified to retrace for you all the steps that had gone before. You listen for a while, until you decide that you have caught the tenor of the argument; then you put in your oar. Someone answers; you answer him; another comes to your defense; another aligns himself against you, to either the embarrassment or gratification of your opponent, depending upon the quality of your ally's assistance. However, the discussion is interminable. The hour grows late, you must depart. And you do depart, with the discussion still vigorously in progress.[5]

---

* This assignment was first developed by Jaclyn Vasquez for the University Writing Program at the University of California, Riverside.

During the COVID-19 pandemic, I taught this assignment over three online quarters. Had I been able to teach the assignment in person, I would have selected two or three students to stand outside the room for five minutes while I gave the remaining students a topic to discuss—something along the lines of *Do you believe the Harry Potter series is sexist?* or *How do standardized tests benefit some more than others?* After five minutes, I would welcome back the students in the hallway without giving them context, advising the students in the classroom to carry on their conversations. They would then live out the parlor story in real time.

Outside of an academic setting, perhaps around one of the tables in the Adult Fiction section at Northwest One, or at the dinner party of a wealthy businessman, the metaphor unfolds in an innumerable number of ways depending on who is present and what their individual experiences and, perhaps, expertise are. But the core of its point remains in any setting: before we enter into a new conversation, before we speak, even if we are an expert in the topic, there is a necessary pause. There is a necessity to listening. In American culture, we often jump right to inserting our oars, sometimes using that oar to splash water on everyone around us so that they might either listen to us more or become so distracted from their own points, their own rowing, that they invest their energy into disagreeing with us, joining us, or arguing against us even more vehemently. There is a certain kind of freedom, then, in a profession where a level of neutrality is expected of you as a public-facing professional. At home in my private life, away from the library, I could easily disappear into off- and online consensus or discord, but in my library work, I had to do my best to interact objectively with any idea that came to the circulation desk. While this was an unspoken requirement for forty hours a week in my role as librarian, outside of the library I still slipped into combative discussions, both off-line and on, where I sought to be "right." This speaks to the incredible pull and pleasure of binary thinking, of having a say in what is right and wrong and who, or what, is good or bad.

I used this particular assignment to remind students that when we begin research, we first must listen and observe to understand what the "conversation" is about. We have to collect the pulse of the topic. Only after that can we begin to truly make assessments, to analyze and synthesize what we have taken in. The very last step in the process, not the reactionary first, is to insert our metaphorical oar.

After I introduce this idea of the parlor lens I ask my students, most of them recent high school graduates, to pick a hashtag on Twitter and answer a series of questions about the larger conversation surrounding it. I ask that they provide the overall context—what users are saying in general about the topic, what sides are being taken—and then identify a few contributors to the different sides of the conversation. They choose one person who they see as contributing productively to the conversation and explain how and why that person is doing so (To inform? To entertain? To elicit an emotional response?). I also ask them to identify a participant in the conversation who is a troll, again asking the same questions of *how* and *why*. The final task of the assignment is to "insert their oar": Where do they stand in the conversation? Have they gained enough knowledge to effectively participate and contribute to the conversation? If not, what could they do to continue their investigation? Students almost always enjoy the assignment, regularly stating that they don't usually think critically about Twitter or similar platforms in these ways, and I in turn, am often impressed by their insight and responses.

The last time I gave this assignment, in early 2021, one student responded to the final questions with this: "Some people take advantage of social media and they tend to diminish people's opinion and that should not be the case. Social media was made so that we could hear both sides and make our own opinion rather than try to force others into thinking what you are thinking."

This response sent me into a spiral of thinking that lasted for days.

Twitter, and other social media, was perhaps originally created so that we could hear many sides, perspectives, and experiences, but this is certainly no longer its primary function. Social media is made and used for reaction, for opinion, for emotional validation, and ultimately for profit. Users are pulled in, again and again, by its allure. But they are not, I would argue, taking in much real information, especially if we consider information in the context of the parlor metaphor. Some social media users show up to the parlor late without the full context and are responding to vague, unexamined, or lazily examined *pieces* of information that are detached from a larger whole. And this make sense—many users are addicted, by design, to the *feeling* of connectivity that social media offers—a feeling that it's not quite fair to call "unreal" or "imagined," but one that is so fractured and expansive it is impossible to ever fully engage with it, no matter how many hours we spend on it.

The rapid-fire flow of short, quippy "takes" we find on Instagram, Twitter, and the like also changes and rearranges how we process the passing of time. Despite our talk of posts happening in "real time," we seem to have lost track of what *real time* even means. In a 2019 BuzzFeed piece titled "The 2010s Broke Our Sense of Time,"[6] Katherine Miller examines our use of technology throughout the decade, ultimately concluding that algorithmic time—a term I use here to discuss how social media companies are able to disseminate posts, giving the appearance of a logical, chronological order—so disorients us because everything "good, bad, and complicated" flows through our phones. The algorithms of Instagram, Twitter, and similar platforms are never with us in the moment; even if you catch a photo during the first seconds it appears online and comment, "First!" the moment of the photo has passed, especially if it's a #tbt or paid collaboration. The same can be said for Internet commentary happening as a story is still breaking. No one has *ever* gotten all the information at once. This is not to say that algorithms rule us or that humans do not have enough autonomy to disengage. They do not and we absolutely do. But the younger a person is, the more likely it is that they have been raised on this type of information intake and two-sided online posting. It is understandable, then, that they might operate within these frameworks thinking all of it is real and in real time, that there is one right way and one wrong way and they must align themselves with one. While scrolling, we can go from feeling elated to terrible within seconds depending on whom we follow, whom we lurk, what the algorithm has offered, and how long we choose to engage. And social media, we now more fully know, is designed to keep us engaged with it. As Miller puts it, "The thing you must say, the thing you've been waiting for—it's always there, pulling you back under again and again and again. Who can remember anything anymore?"

There is the very real fact that we need not give so much power to "the algorithms" because ultimately, we humans have the absolute power to delete our accounts, refuse to engage, and turn off our phones. It is just becoming harder and harder to choose to do those things. In 1991 social psychologist Kenneth Gergen warned of a world like this in his book *The Saturated Self.*[7] A world where advancements in technology could saturate human beings to the point of fragmented versions of the self. A self pulled in so many directions that the original individual becomes lost—drawn and quartered into numerous and competing relationships, projects, and commitments at once, inevitably leaving a person with a pervasive sense of inadequacy.

He writes:

> One detects amid the hurly-burly of contemporary life a new constellation of feelings or sensibilities, a new pattern of self-consciousness. This syndrome may be termed multiphrenia, generally referring to the splitting of the individual into a multiplicity of self-investments. This condition is partly an outcome of self-population, but partly a result of the populated self's efforts to exploit the potentials of the technologies of the relationship. . . . As one's potentials are expanded by the technologies, so one increasingly employs the technologies for self-expression; yet, as the technologies are further utilized, so do they add to the repertoire of potentials. . . . Someday there may indeed be nothing to distinguish multiphrenia from simply "normal living."

More than thirty years later, we can see how Gergen's book reads as something like a prophecy. Many of us have already become afflicted by the syndrome he coined *multiphrenia*, becoming individuals split into a multiplicity of self-investments so numerous that we become more online persona than individual, more present on the Internet and absent in our actual lives. This certainly happens on a spectrum, with some people on a more extreme end, accumulating upwards of eight hours a day of screen time, and others only checking in periodically. We can see how the notion of multiphrenia has permeated our culture. How so many of us struggle to take in information—to process, analyze, and use our understandings of it—for good, for better, for change, and with a lens of curiosity and openness intact. We are all somewhat fragmented, split between our obligations, desires, needs, and wants, in ways that sometimes make it impossible to consider the collective over the individual. We have never been more connected, more bound to a virtual reality, than we are now. Our daily lives have been digitized and tracked, and are tied up in, and by, digital metrics. But our real selves have split—into profile pictures and status updates, hot takes and pithy political positions, ever-changing denouncements and acceptance. And while social media sites do offer a feeling, and sometimes the realness, of community and connectivity, they have also altered our collective understandings of both time and reality in ways that are difficult to undo.

The full impact of social media on our lives is still being examined, but in my own research, I became particularly curious about the growth of cancel culture, a term that has swiftly changed meaning over the last few years. One entry to understanding its evolution is examining the beginning of Twitter threads. While conversation threading—linking a series of messages or thoughts, oldest first—is not new (think e-mail chains and message boards), it is newer on social media. Dan Baum was one of the first and most memorable to use threads in 2009 when he tweeted more than one hundred times to a single thread (with tweets that at the time were limited to 140 characters) over three days about being let go from the *New Yorker*.[8] Around the same time, nineteen-year-old Aziah "Zola" Wells tweeted a 148-tweet thread about going to Florida with a "white bitch" named Jessica who had an overbearing boyfriend. Many Twitter users followed the saga, captivated, including me.[9]

The practice of threading became more and more popular, and today, we see everyone from online astrologers to journalists using the technique to gather information, promote their work, and "build community." We also see it used to "cancel" with lengthy threads unpacking a person's, or persons', wrongdoings. In an online ecosystem that culture writer Lyz Lenz has described as "ruled by likes and retweets,"[10] nothing really *has* to be true, and this leaves the space for everything and anything to be. Extreme weight, and notoriety, can be given to a blue check mark's confirmation of vague legitimacy (though Twitter added more strict guidelines for receiving or keeping the blue check in 2021 and began removing it from users who did not meet the criteria) or an Instagram user's one hundred thousand followers. But these check marks and numbers do not mean that what's being shared is factual or has good intentions. As

Lenz also astutely noted about life after Trump left office, America had begun to "recover from a media cycle that revolved, endlessly, around a cruel and vindictive White House," reminding us of how easily we let conspiracy leak into our lives through TV shows, punditry, and our own thinking. Lenz writes: "How quickly we smashed the retweet button, how little we thought about it. And how dangerous it is to live in a world built entirely of your own words, with no vetting, no editing, blocking critics, until everything is a mirror shining you back at you."

This concept of a mirror shining you back at you can be seen clearly within the broader scope(s) of cancel culture.

In my research, I started with the evolution of the word *cancel* as we apply it culturally and socially. In the past, we have seen terms like *politically correct* and *woke* undergo a similar degradation that *cancel* has undergone in the last few years, a process sometimes referred to as *semantic bleaching*. Semantic bleaching occurs when a word's intensity or meaning lessens because of a change in semantics (its connotation, interpretation, etc.), blurring the conventional use of the word and usually taking it from its community of origin to the mainstream. (As with much of the current American lexicon, the word *cancel* [and *woke* and many, many others] was adapted from Black culture. In 2013 and 2014 the word *cancel* was used among younger people online, in particular on Black Twitter,[11] as a word closer to being synonymous with *boycott*— not giving attention, money, support, time, and so forth, to a particular person or organization because of their actions or inactions.) Journalist Aja Romano found what might be considered the first popular reference to *cancel* or *canceling* as applied to individuals, not things, in the 1991 movie *New Jack City*. In the film, lead character and crime boss Nino Brown (played by Wesley Snipes) slams his girlfriend down on a table and spills champagne over her saying, "Cancel that bitch. I'll buy another one." Two other men look on, and as she yells, "I hate you, Nino! I hate you!" she is removed from the room by one of them.

While this denotation of the word *cancel* has continued shifting since this first iteration of it in the 1990s, the general concept of *canceling* a person is nothing new. Public shaming of people who have been deemed moral transgressors has been around for centuries, from the book of Leviticus's scapegoat, to seventeenth-century whippings and stockades, to the Salem witch trials, to Hester Prynne's scarlet *A*. Shaming has been utilized for centuries to draw a line between good and bad, us and them. These days, shaming often looks like a form of collective actions—the initial call out, Twitter threading, Instagram infographic posting, calls to action, posts and videos from victims, and so forth—and is most frequently conducted on social media before it reaches the broader media.

What I find most interesting about our modernized use of the word *cancel* is that it is used in debates that are essentially about the best ways for societies to be inclusive and protective. But these actions and conversations often lead to divisiveness instead, usually between one group who believes the transgressor deserves some leniency and another who wants the transgressor essentially erased from existence. While there is a spectrum and plenty of room for nuance around cancel culture and who is, or isn't, canceled, rarely does social media foster that nuance by accepting someone expressing opinions that fall somewhere in the middle.

Writer Ligaya Mishan credits our modern concept of canceling to a collective loss of faith in the ability or desire of institutions to uphold what is good, writing, "If you no longer believe that we live in a city upon a hill, that our society is just or even aspires to be—there may be no recourse (short of revolution) but to scold and menace, like modern-day Puritans."[12] Our inclusivity still derives from community agreed-on standards, but as these standards have become increasingly automatized, it makes it virtually impossible to adhere to all of them, all the time, or to even know what many of them are. But still, when someone does not meet a standard or standards, especially more resolute, developed, and agreed-on ones, canceling occurs. This creation of new standards, and of canceling those who do not follow them, has in many ways enabled marginalized voices to be heard in new ways. Anne Charity Hudley, who holds an endowed chair in the linguistics of African America at the University of California, Santa Barbara, has powerfully noted that "canceling is a way to acknowledge that you don't have to have the power to change structural inequality. You don't even have to have the power to change all of public sentiment. But as an individual, you can still have power beyond measure. . . . When you see people canceling Kanye, canceling other people, it's a collective way of saying, 'We elevated your social status, your economic prowess, [and] we're not going to pay attention to you in the way that we once did. . . . I may have no power, but the power I have is to [ignore] you.'"[13]

I remain most curious about *who* has power taken from them by the acts of canceling. Some targets of cancel culture are singled out among others who have committed comparable transgressions, allowing for something like a Shirley Jackson "Lottery"–level ritualistic cruelty where participants turn on their (in Jackson's story, randomly selected) kind. This is, at least in part, because it is easier to identify a scapegoat than it is to look inward and recognize that who, and what, you are denouncing is not always so removed from yourself. In his book *A Secular Age*, Canadian philosopher Charles Taylor[14] writes of how this person (who he refers to as a scapegoat), whether guilty or not of a specific offense, is ultimately a stand-in for the true culprits responsible for a *society* gone askew. A society, and system, that we ourselves are complicit in. Scapegoats are demonized, forced to bear and personify everyone's guilt on top of their own, while the system continues to thrive.

One example of a scapegoat as Taylor defines it is the woman who called the police on the Central Park bird-watcher in the spring of 2020. She was rightfully condemned for her racist actions, actions that embodied a much larger social problem. This does not mean she did not deserve to be called out, only that her actions were captured, shared, and caused anger and rage that many others who behaved, or behave, similarly have escaped, oftentimes by sheer luck. She took on the rage of many people who were angry not just at her, but at a larger system.

Celebrities, and more public-facing individuals, embody something else. People like Louis C.K., Aziz Ansari, Logan Paul, and Erykah Badu—all mentioned in a 2018 *New York Times* piece called "Everyone is Canceled"[15]—have supposedly been canceled. And yet they continue to be alive, well, and prosperous today, often with even more supportive audiences than before they were canceled. As Mishan smartly writes: "So long as the folk devils of cancel culture are plucked from the masses or are merely artsy celebrities or subalterns of politics or industry, the world stays essentially the same."[16]

What we might consider a pathway away from the fragmentation and individualism, the scapegoating and straw-manning, that has been stoked by modern technology and social media is what I saw again and again at the library, particularly at the circulation desk. A willingness to engage with a sense of curiosity and openness so that we might not just find common ground but also better understand opposing views, experiences, struggles, and mistakes as well.

In the complex day-to-day happenings of Northwest One, patrons also sat together at tables and spoke to each other about their lives, their views, their beliefs. When violent incidents occurred, they checked in with each other and with library workers. They helped us pick up thrown items, and they asked if we were OK. They tended to each other, they protected each other's privacy, they noticed when they hadn't seen someone for a while. We coexisted to the best of all our abilities not in some false utopia but in the very reality of each other's humanness. Offensive things were said and done, boundaries were sometimes crossed, across every relationship in the library—patron to patron, coworker to coworker, patron to library worker, library worker to patron—and each time, the struggle to protect the library space remained. Sometimes people were barred, sometimes fights erupted, and sometimes everyone reentered the same space the next day and found a way to coexist. Although I have written here about what the ultimate empathy fatigue and burnout being in this environment led to for me, I also understand this to be about systemic failure more than it was ever about individual human beings. As author and scientist Robin Wall Kimmerer writes in her book *Braiding Sweetgrass* about humans' reciprocal relationship with the rest of the world, "The more something is shared, the greater its value becomes."[17] Kimmerer goes on to say that this concept "is hard to grasp for societies steeped in notions of private property, where others are, by definition, excluded from sharing." Most patrons I saw on a daily basis at Northwest One were excluded from sharing, often because of one or more reasons like race, gender, or socioeconomic status that were largely outside of their immediate control. But the library, as so many note, was the one free place they could go to freely. That invited them to also share.

What better examples of human-to-human, community-member-to-community-member sharing in American society, for better and worse, do we have than our public libraries? From their earliest to their most modern forms, libraries share. Not just books and other resources, but human interactions. As I've noted, many demographics have been excluded from this access, and many demographics continue to have subpar libraries based on where they live. But all people are welcome to public libraries so long as they follow certain stated rules and basic usage agreements.

That the majority of American citizens support public libraries—whether by regularly patronizing them, financially supporting their funding and existence, or something in between—gives me a deep sense of hope that we still fundamentally believe in sharing.

And yet we have, collectively, strayed from that understanding. You need only visit your local library and watch who patronizes it, and in what ways, to see a living, breathing embodiment of what happens when we strip people of their basic humanities, often based on race, gender, sexual orientation, and socioeconomic status. It is what keeps many people I know out of public libraries or limits their usage to picking up books they've put on hold. It is what my friends with children struggle to introduce to their young children—that some people have so much and some people have so little and we all live in the same place.

Here is where I see the real light of the library. Not the light that Carnegie and other early library founders waxed poetic about; the light they believed libraries would give the public through free access, which they etched into its earliest walls, but did not mean for all. The actual light that libraries provide comes not just from the books and resources and shared resources but from the people within them and the stories they carry—both the library workers and the patrons. That light beams that we can care for others more justly, equally, and empathetically. That we can do so without tying it to capitalism, to profit and commodity. That we might all have a willingness to bolster and create shared free spaces, customs, and broadly accepted societal beliefs that we all have inherent rights as human beings. Hope for a more holistic, transparent, forgiving, and supportive communal world. Public libraries show us how to come back to so much of what we have lost, so much of what we collectively feel aching and missing, if we take the time to look.

There was no looking away at Northwest One. Not from the impacts of wealth inequality, inadequate health care, racism, addiction, and policing.

Not from humans in pain who were struggling and lashing out. Not from the small, joyful, and often unexpected moments of connection and humanity that happened too. Reckoning with our humanity happened daily. All who shared the space of Northwest One coexisted with each other, to the best of our abilities, in a way that many Americans with certain levels of privilege often opt not to.

Despite the possibility for, and the ease of, avoidance or denial, we remain connected. Regardless of developing technologies or passing time, regardless of cultural trends and shifts, of deciding who is right and who is wrong, who belongs and who does not, everything—everyone—remains connected.

What I see here, in our collective struggle to take in information (and then to make deliberate and meaningful change from our assessments *before* developing our opinions or taking stances), in our constant efforts to better define, or redefine, our norms and boundaries, in our struggles to reckon with many pieces of our history, in our struggles to see and understand and witness and perhaps help one another, is a growing opportunity for collective empathy, change, and growth. And in all of that, I see hope of the deepest kind.

12

THE FUTURE OF
THE AMERICAN
PUBLIC LIBRARY

All that you Change
Changes you.
The only lasting truth
is Change.

—Octavia E. Butler, *Parable of the Sower*

HOPE IS WHAT I REFER TO as a *sweeping word*. I call it *sweeping* because
it usually involves sweeping something deeply complex into a singular
vague meaning. Not quite semantic bleaching, but some other degradation. This brand of *hope* gets wielded the most these days by Instagram
influencer televangelists, sitting alongside words like *grace, tenderness,* and
peace that are intended to embody whole ways of living as they gloss over
systemic realities. They are words they tell people to "sit with" or "journal
about" but never what to do with them next when they stand back up.
The *hope* I mean was taught to me by my mother, who was taught it by
her own mother.

My grandmother, Wilma K. Rapp, was born in 1927, two years before
the beginning of the Great Depression and less than a decade after the
influenza pandemic. She grew up on a farm in rural western New York,

attended a one-room schoolhouse, and raised eight children while working full-time as a nurse in a Buffalo hospital. As of this writing, she is ninety-three years old and still sends me holiday and birthday cards addressed to "Mandi." Inside are always short notes that catch me by some invisible fishhook and pull me back to being younger and softer.

The hope I was taught by my grandmother and my mother began with anxiety and fear, and I don't personally think that's a bad place for hope to begin.

Bear with me as I attempt to describe the overall feeling of not belonging in childhood, something that nearly everyone experiences at one age or another but still feels deeply personal to each of us. I don't know anyone who can't think of a physical feature or a first crush or a bully whose memory doesn't still grab them by the face in the mirror sometimes. And we still, privately and quietly, have to remind ourselves that we are not that little person anymore with huge glasses and braces, the one not cool enough to be worthy of the popular boy's attention, or whatever individual brand of not belonging it is that belongs to us.

What haunted my middle school days was an overall anxiety about fitting in. Part of it came from a socioeconomic gap between me and most of my classmates, and part of it came from the ways I was born and raised. I wanted people to like me, and I was trying to figure out what currency that took, who took it, how much of it I had, and how much I still needed to earn. I worried daily that my friends at school would stop talking to me because I was not cool enough—I didn't have the right hair, or shoes, or interests, or clothes. This looming, and mostly unfounded, fear of rejection and abandonment kept me anxious most hours of the school day and kept me up at night, even though there were, as my father says, *bigger fish to fry*.

Once after I had a particularly brutal day of fifth-grade emotions, my mother sat on the end of my twin bed and told me what her own mother had once told her about worrying: Whatever it is you're worried about, imagine the very worst that can happen. Go deep down that worst-case-scenario rabbit hole and come up with the very worst of it besides it killing you. Feel it, imagine it, name it, and really think of that worst thing.

"Then," she'd say, "work backward."

I went to bed that night thinking about how it would feel to show up to school and have everyone shun me in a complete and total fifth-grade rejection. This was my worst fear then, the kind that made me feel physically ill. I lingered there for a while, feeling how deeply afraid I was that it would happen, feeling how bad it would be. And then eventually, I felt ready to try what my grandmother and mother had recommended. I worked backward.

Could I survive that? Yes, even if it was painful, having no friends would not kill me.

How likely was it that no one would ever talk to me again? It was almost impossible. The school would intervene at some point. And my friends Missy and Heather would never really turn their backs on me.

Were there others like them? Yes.

I named everyone I thought might not go with the consensus, might still be my friend, and then I kept going:

Could I survive with two or three good friends? Yes.

Did I want to be more popular? Yes.

Was my real fear that I wasn't ever going to have a big group of friends? Probably.

Would it really be that bad if I never did? Probably not.

Would it most likely end up being a little better than that? Definitely.

There was immense relief that came from letting myself imagine the worst-case scenario and then working my way back up from it. I'd faced my fifth-grade version of rock bottom, realized it probably wouldn't come true, and felt freer and safer to begin thinking of ways to come back up and handle the reality.

This is the hope I mean.

The kind that comes from looking, thinking, grappling, even obsessing—often with anxiety or fear—about possible outcomes and then working backward until it feels possible again to imagine something less terrifying.

It was difficult to apply this matriarchal advice to my work at Northwest One. Imagining worst-case scenarios was futile, as worst-case scenarios often played out and sometimes in ways worse than I could imagine. A patron overdosed, teenagers fought violently, an entire family slept outside the library in their car and woke there each morning. Worst-case scenarios existed in and around the library constantly, directly and tangentially. My experience of, and proximity to, so much worst-case scenario took a core piece from me. I lost hope at the library. I lost my ability to work backward.

In the 2016 edition of her book *Hope in the Dark*, Rebecca Solnit includes an afterword where she speaks to the hope that she has seen emulated by people of color in even the most dire circumstances, people like Mexican Zapatistas, survivors of Pol Pot's regime, and undocumented Haitian, Latino, and Maya immigrants who fought for farmworkers' rights. She then notes that middle-class White people often don't know how to be these kinds of people—people who lack bitterness, even though they have the most right to it, and "could speak of big dreams, of high ideals, of deep emotion." A middle-class White woman herself, she writes, "I've met so many of my kind who are attached for various reasons to their limits and their misery."[1]

When I worked at Northwest One, I was attached to my personal limits and misery and to the limits and misery I found in the work. I had that—what I can only think to call—privilege. Privilege to go deep into despair and then to walk away from what felt like the root of it. To quit. Self-flagellation is not something I am interested in performing here or anywhere else, but I still sometimes wish I had been a different person. The kind who stayed in the work and found hope there, again. I lost hope and I left. And when I did, I could not imagine finding a return to the working backward.

I ultimately owe a great deal of my personal growth and evolution to the library. To the patrons and my coworkers, all of whom I feel immeasurably deep respect and care for. It has only been through honest reflection and reckoning about my time as a librarian, through thinking and researching and writing this book, that my hope-finding process eventually returned. That I am again able to face possible outcomes and then, much more importantly, future realities. I have spent every day since leaving Northwest One regaining that hope, and I have had the privilege of time, space, access, and safety to do so. My imagined worst worst-case scenarios are of course much broader now than they were when I was a child, but they are also more layered and expansive than during my time at Northwest One. I left the library, library work, and DC in September 2018. No part of me then imagined the political unrest that was still to come, or that a pandemic would close public libraries down for weeks and months. I had not imagined, even at my most cynical moments, a scenario where public libraries all over the world closed their physical doors. Where so much of the world outside suffered.

In the early days of the pandemic, a coworker from the library sent me a photo from outside Northwest One. The DC Public Library, like library systems all over the country, had shuttered its branches in late March 2020. The photo showed patrons, some of whom I recognized, sleeping outside the branch on the ground. However bad the pandemic was for me and so many others, what it would have been like without stable shelter and care seems—and for many *was*—insurmountable. The number of unhoused people who died from COVID-19 is unknown, but there are pieces of information that have been gathered: shelters all over the country had outbreaks and restricted capacity, forcing people back out onto the streets; social services and harm-reduction programs remained closed or lessened services for months; and in New York, the mortality rate of unhoused people was 75 percent higher than the city's rate.[2] Beyond this, most of what we know is minimal, and I have read article after article that refers to unhoused people as "the uncounted" in COVID-19 death statistics.

Northwest One was a small and complicated branch in a large city. It was one public library among twenty-six in DC and thousands within America. But it was a lifeline to hundreds of people every single day. One worst-case scenario for Northwest One was that it would close, and like so many worst-case scenarios involving the branch, it came to fruition. Around the same time my coworker sent the photo, I learned that Northwest One might never reopen, and I hit my lowest emotional point of quarantine and the pandemic in part because I could not stop thinking about the patrons of Northwest One.

As spring ended and death tolls continued to rise, I began the painful work of finding hope again, alone in my studio apartment in Riverside, California. I began to imagine that billionaires would take over the world even more than they already have, that democracy—whatever version of it we now have—would continue to devolve, that despair, defeatism, and cynicism would grow, climate change would drown cities, and even more species would be wiped out. That nowhere would be safe or easily inhabited, and with the rest of the most noble American institutions, libraries would disappear altogether.

I let myself stay there, in that despair and excruciating sadness that has felt easier and easier to disappear into with each passing year. I realize and accept, at least on an intellectual level, that all of this has already come to be, at least in part, and much of it will only get worse based on our current trajectory.

I spent many of the spring months of 2020 crying about it, feeling angry about it, calling my parents, my brother, my closest friends. I tweeted about it, I posted about it, I called on some higher power I have never believed in. And when I was done putting it out into the imagined and real world, I sat alone with it.

And then eventually, as weeks and months passed, as the care I had taken for and with myself after leaving library work continued to echo, I started to work backward again.

I am still working backward.

I look at what happened and didn't happen in the immediate and then long-term aftermath of COVID-19, how many people died and how many of them did without their loved ones nearby; how many grieved those losses without the possibility of gathering to support one another, to hold each other and be held. I think of the sheer and overwhelming amount of human loss and of how many people have not yet begun to process it and how so many may never do so. I think about the "uncounted" and feel physically ill. I think of how the rich got ever richer and the poor became more impoverished, how people were forced to go back to work under unsafe conditions, how librarians weren't given vaccine priority in many states despite their first-responder designations, and on and on and on, until finally, I feel able to ask questions again.

Did some people start to care more about understanding social injustices during COVID-19? Yes. Did community involvement and activism increase, did the terms *autonomous mutual aid* come more into the mainstream and become better understood and supported? Yes. Did I see friends and family leave stagnant, thankless jobs, relationships, locations, lives? Yes. Did thousands, if not millions, of people begin to come deeper into a reckoning with systemic racism in our country? Yes.

Are there many who did not? Yes. Does that mean they never will? No.

Are our politics still mired in the racist ideals of Jim Crow? Yes. Is housing inequality rampantly growing? Yes. Is higher education still gatekept? Yes.

But might so many people's anger with social inequalities be proof of how much they care about surviving, about survival, and might it go beyond themselves and their family and friends and out to their community? Could our sadness and fear begin to be understood as knowledge that we are all connected in spirit? Aren't we taking some of that energy and turning it toward good already? Isn't it possible that we will not just put up with less injustice but begin to infuse our culture—our K–12 schools, our higher-education institutions, our family dinners, our gatherings with friends—with planning about how we might most impactfully do so? Haven't we seen again and again that people revert to care and resourcefulness in crisis?

I sit in all of that too. And I regularly check the pulse of what feels the most frightening about our past, present, and future. This process is continual. Every one of my affirmative answers comes with pushback. For each positive, there is usually also a negative. For every wound healed, there are always more that need attention. Sometimes I am exhausted. And sometimes I allow myself days and weeks of not thinking about the worst of it; I still want to shield myself from the worst of it sometimes. But I also know the overarching truth remains constant, regardless of my willingness to face it, that with every desire to protect ourselves from facing a raw truth, we miss an opportunity to begin to learn from it. When we don't ask questions, when we move from feelings of defeat to actions of being defeated, when we remain stagnant, we cannot find answers. We cannot find hope.

The hope I mean offers us a certain clarity. It reminds us of our shared reality, in its truest forms. It comes with the vulnerable and deeply human and humane ability to say, "I don't know yet, but I am going to keep seeking and learning and trying." It is a commitment to moving forward instead of staying stuck in guilt or anger, instead of remaining perpetually in grief. This hope does not rely on old ideas or incomplete truths, like the notion that the library can "save" us. That kind of salvation defers the possibility of change to *elsewhere*—some higher power, some person or entity who might respond to our prayer with deliverance—and allows us to remain passive in our fate and in the fate of others. Faith keeps us from despair and cynicism, but it is hope that calls us to action. It moves us to reckon with and understand the past and present for what it is, to the best of our abilities, so that we can keep moving in all directions, no matter the fear about how much work might come next. No matter the fear of how it might be. Regardless of the anguish it sometimes causes, hope asks us to look.

I saw this kind of fear, one rooted in looking away, immobilize managers and administrators and my coworkers at the DC Public Library again and again. I see this fear immobilize so many other institutions and communities and individuals as well. It is rooted in not wanting to look at what most overwhelms and hurts us, and also not wanting to make mistakes, not wanting to be "wrong." Binary thinking often feels easier. It removes a layer—of guilt, of anguish, of error, of heartbreak, of doubt. But it also removes the most tender, in-tune, and caring parts of us.

This fear is rooted in capitalist ideas of time and value: that there is not enough, that we are not enough, that we cannot do more with what we know. This fear overwhelms everything, unless we don't let it.

I find hope here, again. In this acknowledgment that hope absolutely always coexists with pain and tumult and, sometimes, deep suffering. That feelings of defeat, sadness, anger, and all of those more complex emotions that exist beyond "good" or "bad" are not incompatible with, or contrary to, hope. They are part of it also. Fear is an access point to hope if we approach it correctly.

What we might consider the exact opposite of fear is the blind optimism that often delays, if not destroys, hope. It takes away its autonomy, its possibility, and all the potential solutions we might find by sitting in the worst of it. As James Baldwin wrote, "Not everything that is faced can be changed, but nothing can be changed until it is faced."[3] Hope comes from looking at something head-on. It is not pure optimism. It is not willful ignorance or refusing to reflect or "think negatively." It is a deep, intrinsic belief in our ability to move forward, in action. Hope is, above all else, an action. To powerfully reach that side of it, we often have to recognize the worst of something first before we can come up with how to move forward. When we look harder at the cracks in our society, we can also begin to see the resilience and resistance. We can begin to see an embodied call, and a demand, for care. In seeing what is broken, we can see all that is not broken too.

The day after the 2017 mass shooting in Las Vegas, author and activist adrienne maree brown posted to her blog:

> we must, each of us, fix our attention on the nearest wound, conjure within us the smallest parts of ourselves that are still whole, and be healers. there's enough destruction. there's enough nothingness swallowing the living world. don't add to it. there's enough.[4]

While everything I have ever read by brown is impactful, the idea of the *nearest wound* has stayed with me in ways that only a handful of other quotes have. When I think about libraries, I think about places that hold people who try to do just that. I am referring less to the library workers than to the patrons.

I made sure to open this book by stating that I am in no way a voice for the voiceless. I do not believe a voiceless person exists—only people who are ignored or otherwise silenced. But I would be mistaken if I did not note that all the patrons I saw at Northwest One, even the ones I had difficult interactions with, were trying to address the nearest wounds, whatever they were. I saw it when they lent each other cell phones and change, when they bickered over politics, when they guarded each other's belongings. I saw it when they refused to tell on each other for breaking the library rules, and I saw it when they relied on substances to get through every waking minute of every day. I saw it when they yelled, fought, demanded. The patrons at Northwest One knew what it meant to resist being swallowed by the world. When I suggest that we might emulate libraries and librarians, I suggest, too, that we would be well served to emulate the grit and care of their most vulnerable patrons as well. Their hope is some of the strongest I have ever witnessed.

When I see what I see—which is usually a long line of questions—I recognize all the people who might have answers to how we make our world better. Who might also have even better questions than me. There are thousands, if not hundreds of thousands, of people who are better at the job of librarian than I was. There are the people who stay in library work who have more patience, grit, and expertise than me, who don't just find bits of joy in the work, but mountains of it. They imagine and see so much more than I do. There is always something others can imagine that we cannot. Young people who are not yet thinking about a career but love the library. High school students who get service hours in the library after school. People just entering MLS programs or just graduating from them. Patrons who spend their days in libraries and have ideas for what would make them even better. People who have no interest in being a librarian but who are passionate about some other field that they can immerse themselves in and help others through. Humans who care about animals and plants and the world around them and want to read about it, write about it, protect it. Humans who crave conversation, forgiveness, understanding, reparations, alleviation.

In her enigmatic book *Água Viva*, Clarice Lispector writes, "At the bottom of everything there is the hallelujah."[5] I think of all of this—all this possibility, all this reckoning with what has happened, what remains, and what might still happen—as the hallelujah.

I am just beginning to feel happy when I see something about how we "need libraries" or "libraries will save us." I'm not so focused now on the ramifications of an incomplete understanding of libraries, not already mad and thinking about how what's asked of them is insurmountable. Instead, I find myself feeling more and more glad that we believe that something like a library *can* save us. That most American citizens support public libraries and continue to hold them in high esteem.

To answer the lingering question of *What about their future?* I believe libraries will exist as long as humans do. No matter how dire the worst-case scenario we work back from, this is a future I can predict resolutely. That libraries will always be needed, patronized, and, if we're lucky, cherished.

I can, and do, imagine a future where the light of the library touches everyone the way it first promised to over two hundred years ago. I can imagine a future where, when someone makes a mistake, they say it plainly and fix it fully through restorative justice models or some other intentional process.

I can imagine a future where every city or town or community has community fridges that are regularly stocked. That the people who stock them have spent time meeting and getting to know the people who use them. Where all have engaged in long conversations to learn the spectrum of each other's needs and limits and concerns, commonalities and differences, and fully experience the heartbreak of sharing a world where some people have enough to eat and some do not. I can imagine a future where that makes people move forward differently than before. I can imagine a future where everyone has housing. Where all of us suddenly appear more clearly as individuals to each other, individuals who have unique upbringings and life experiences that influence how we think, and that we remain open and curious in our actions like a librarian at a circulation desk. That no one believes one person is inherently *bad*. That we might work together to see how those differences, together, would make for a better collective world.

I can imagine a future where people engage through lenses of curiosity and empathy, not revenge or anger or dominance. Not with a priority, above all else, to be "right." I can imagine a future that allows space for individuals and institutions to examine their pasts, and their mistakes, more truthfully, with a restorative or reparative process in place.

I can envision a future where libraries are one of *many* institutions leading the way toward communal compassion. Where libraries are still needed, but not essential to so many people for basic care and survival. A future where more people understand the many ways we—all of us— need each other. Where people advocate for more library-like services in their communities.

Even in my worst imagined barren world that is torn apart by climate change and displacement and lack of resources, I still see some versions of libraries. I see books and information and people who keep and protect it. I see you, book in hand, sitting here reading, and I wonder what you might do next. I wonder how you might find real, actionable hope and how you might reach more of it. I can imagine this as well—and the many possibilities for the better that it might create.

I can imagine these things in large part because I worked in a library. Because I was a librarian in a complicated city full of dichotomies and rich histories, failures and deep transgressions, and I got to know a community there intimately. Because that closeness cracked me open and I ran away. Because I came back eventually to reckon with what I learned and am still learning.

What I know for certain is this: our true nature—the physiological, foundational *stuff* that has allowed us to evolve—is steeped in community, in empathy and care and understanding for each other. That is how we have survived. That is how we will continue to survive. However many outside forces fragment us or pull us from our most inherent senses of ourselves and each other, from our sense of place and the natural world, we remain deeply connected. And we remain, too, deeply capable of using that connection to change things for not just ourselves, but for each other.

Libraries, perhaps above all else, embody this truth.

Every question I have asked and every idea I have posited in these pages has been included with a hope that it might send others down their own paths of research and reckoning, of change. Part of our collective truth—one that has been recorded, housed, and protected for centuries in libraries and by librarians—is that we are all connected to each other. Perhaps the most important part of our collective work now is remembering that. Remembering our inherent relationship to each other, to our planet, and a sense of human duty to both. It requires research and thinking, curiosity and openness. It requires a pause. May libraries shine their light as unending reminders of who we have been and who we might be. May their future be better still than I can imagine.

ACKNOWLEDGMENTS

These pages would have never happened without the support of so many people, but especially Sheri Fink and Vanessa Johnston. Your input, intelligence, encouragement, and care over the years allowed for these pages. To my brother, Joshua Aaron, for all the many ways you have made life and writing more possible for me. To all my family, for being who I come from and where I can return.

My gratitude beyond measure to my agent and friend, Monika Woods, for trusting in this and pushing me to make it better. To my editor, Kara Rota, for your friendship and goodness. I know that might seem a strange thing to thank you for first, but I value this most—that you are also a magnificent editor is the gift of a lifetime. There was no one else for this book. To everyone at Chicago Review Press, for your help in bringing this to life. I am deeply thankful, and proud, this book found its home with you.

My deep appreciation to the faculty at the UC Riverside MFA program, but especially Tom Lutz, Reza Aslan, Emily Rapp Black, Allison Benis White, Katie Ford, and Susan Straight for your help, truth, and kindness. It is the privilege of a lifetime to have learned from each of you. My gratitude to Gil Soltz and the Yefe Nof Residency and Pam Houston and the Mill House Residency, for the much-needed time, space, and beauty you provided.

Thank you to Hannah Hull, my oldest and truest friend, for being part of every story here and for loving me as I am, and as I changed, all these years. Thank you to Justin Danks, for your friendship and the generous ways you made it easier for me to write. To Liv Stratman, for our weekly editing phone calls, without which this book might never have been finished. To those who read early pages, including Amanda Twombly, Jessica Astrella, Dave Depper, Aimee Ortega, Jared Catapano, Chris Scott, and Yena Sharma Purmasir. Thank you to Matthew Astrella, Aimee Buyea, Andy Brown, Patrick Carroll, Lania Cortez, Jeremy DeBottis, Sandy Guttman, Akilah Hughes, Cassie Marketos, Heather Wells Peterson, Zan Romanoff, Crystal Salas, Joe Satran, and Joe Veix for your friendship, care, and thoughts. To all who provided me a quiet space to write, especially Joanna Longe, Robin Hercia, and Joseph McKee.

I have always been a person who asks questions, and I am deeply thankful to all who responded to my questions along the way, including Wayne Wiegand, Alicia Puente Cackley, Leah Esguerra, and many, many others. Thank you to every librarian who spoke with me about your experiences and for being so much of what is so good about libraries.

To DB, TN, and KF: the three of you exist forever in a part of my heart that no one else can ever know as well. There is no one I would have rather worked alongside. And finally, to MR, for all you did for the DC community and Northwest One and for teaching me even when I was not quite ready to learn. Your memory lives on.

NOTES

PART I: BECOMING

1: Northwest One

1   Sarah Nicolas, "50 of Our Favorite Library Quotes About How Awesome Libraries Are," BOOK RIOT, March 8, 2018, https://bookriot.com/library-quotes/.

2   Claire Bushey, "Newsmaker: Judy Blume," *American Libraries*, April 15, 2014, https://americanlibrariesmagazine.org/2014/04/15/newsmaker-judy-blume/.

3   Margaret Atwood (@MargaretAtwood), Twitter, August 1, 2011, 5:11 PM, https://twitter.com/MargaretAtwood/status/98184072043573248.

4   American Library Association, *The State of America's Libraries 2019: A Report from the American Library Association*, ed. Kathy S. Rosa (2019), http://www.ala.org/news/state-americas-libraries-report-2019.

5   American Library Association, *The State of America's Libraries 2020: A Report from the American Library Association*, ed. Steve Zalusky (2020), http://www.ala.org/news/state-americas-libraries-report-2020.

6   American Library Association, *The State of America's Libraries 2019*.

7   Public Library Association (PLA), "Resources for Public Libraries Serving Persons Experiencing Homelessness," March 22, 2019, https://www.ala.org/pla/resources/tools/homelessness.

8   Carl Sagan, *Cosmos* (New York: Random House, 1980).

2: *Omnium lux civium*

1   Benjamin Franklin, *Political, Miscellaneous, and Philosophical Pieces*, ed. Benjamin Vaughan, (London, 1779), 533–536.

2   "About LCP," The Library Company of Philadelphia, https://librarycompany .org/about-lcp/.

3   Donald G. Davis, "Quarter of a Millennium: The Library Company of Philadelphia, 1731–1981: A Symposium, an Exhibition, a Man," *Journal of Library History (1974–1987)* 17, no. 3 (1982): 328–342, http://www.jstor.org /stable/25541294.

4   City Document no. 37, *Report of the Trustees of the Public Library of the City of Boston*, 1852.

5   This letter is excerpted in Walter Muir Whitehill, *Boston Public Library: A Centennial History* (Cambridge, MA: Harvard University Press, 1956), 35, https:// www.boston.gov/sites/default/files/embed/file/2016-11/boston_public_library _central_branch_99.pdf.

6   Paula D. Watson, "Founding Mothers: The Contribution of Women's Organizations to Public Library Development in the United States," *Library Quarterly: Information, Community, Policy* 64, no. 3 (1994): 233–269, www.jstor .org/stable/4308944.

7   Library Bill of Rights, *Advocacy, Legislation and Issues*, June 30, 2006, https:// www.ala.org/advocacy/intfreedom/librarybill.

8   Andrew Carnegie, *The Autobiography of Andrew Carnegie: With Illustrations* (London: Constable, 1920).

9   Howard C. Hill, "The Americanization Movement," *American Journal of Sociology* 24, no. 6 (May 1919): 609–642, https://doi.org/10.1086/212969.

10 Brando Simeo Starkey, "White Immigrants Weren't Always Considered White—and Acceptable," *The Undefeated*, February 10, 2017, https:// theundefeated.com/features/white-immigrants-werent-always-considered -white-and-acceptable/.

11 S. J. Ackerman, "The Trials of S. W. Tucker," *Washington Post*, June 11, 2000, https://www.washingtonpost.com/archive/lifestyle/magazine/2000/06/11 /the-trials-of-sw-tucker/afe63ebe-8e24-4173-9570-0f3cd6ecf2e3/.

12 William B. McClain and Mary Elizabeth Joyce, "How Far to the Promised Land?" (speech), Seventeenth Street Baptist Church, June 24, 2016, Anniston,

AL, https://www.bu.edu/sth/files/2019/09/How-far-the-promised-land -Bobby-McClain.docx.pdf.

13 "ALA Honors African Americans Who Fought Library Segregation," *American Libraries*, July 3, 2018, https://americanlibrariesmagazine.org/blogs /the-scoop/ala-honors-african-americans-who-fought-library-segregation/.

14 "Resolution to Honor African Americans Who Fought Library Segregation," adopted by the Council of the American Library Association June 24, 2018, in New Orleans, Louisiana, http://www.ala.org/aboutala/sites/ala.org.aboutala /files/content/cro/getinvolved/cd-41-Resol-2-Hon-African%20Amers-Who -Fought-%20L-Seg-7618-FINAL%20%28003%29.docx.

15 111th Congress, 1st Session, S. J. Res. 14, https://www.congress.gov/111/bills /sjres14/BILLS-111sjres14is.pdf.

16 Katie Kane, "On WHEREAS by Layli Long Soldier," *Georgia Review*, Fall 2017, https://thegeorgiareview.com/posts/on-whereas-by-layli-long-soldier/.

17 George M. Eberhart, "Desegregating Public Libraries," *American Libraries*, June 25, 2018, https://americanlibrariesmagazine.org/blogs/the-scoop /desegregating-public-libraries/.

18 "Hunger, Homelessness, and Poverty Task Force (HHPTF)," American Library Association, April 26, 2012, http://www.ala.org/rt/srrt/hunger -homelessness-and-poverty-task-force-hhptf.

19 American Library Association, "Hunger, Homelessness, and Poverty Task Force (HHPTF)," Social Responsibilities Round Table, April 26, 2012, http:// www.ala.org/rt/srrt/hunger-homelessness-and-poverty-task-force-hhptf, Document ID: 2a5594fd-08fa-a264-254e-9bf2e08a3efa.

20 *Public Libraries Survey (PLS) Data and Reports*, FY 2015, https://www .oclc.org/content/dam/oclc/reports/awareness-to-funding-2018/2018_From _Awareness_to_Funding_Report.pdf.

21 Lisa Gieskes, "Summary of the ALA Task Force Survey on ALA Policy 61 Library Services for the Poor," accessed March 8, 2020, https://ola.memberclicks .net/assets/SRRT/srrt_policy%2061%20summary%20report.pdf.

22 April Hathcock,. "ALAMW: What Happened, and What Should Happen Next," *At the Intersection* (blog), January 30, 2019, https://aprilhathcock.wordpress .com/2019/01/30/alamw-what-happened-and-what-should-happen-next/.

23 Maria Tumarkin, *Axiomatic*, (Oakland: Transit Books, 2019).

3: So, What Do You Do?

1   Martin Austermuhle and Kate McGee, "D.C. Schools Chancellor Antwan Wilson Resigns After School-Transfer Scandal," WAMU, https://wamu.org /story/18/02/20/d-c-schools-chancellor-antwan-wilson-school-transfer -scandal/.

4: The Library from "L"

1   "Live Smart. Work Smart. Travel Smart.," NoMa Business Improvement District, https://www.nomabid.org/.

2   Tommy Orange, *There There* (New York: Alfred A. Knopf, 2018).

3   Peter Moskowitz, *How to Kill a City: Gentrification, Inequality, and the Fight for the Neighborhood* (New York: Nation Books, 2017).

4   Jeff Chang, *We Gon' Be Alright: Notes on Race and Resegregation* (New York: Picador, 2016).

5   "Macefield Music Festival Rises Where ReverbFest Fell," *Westside Seattle*, https://www.westsideseattle.com/ballard-news-tribune/2013/09/09/macefield -music-festival-rises-where-reverbfest-fell.

PART II: EMPATHY

5: Can You Help Me?

1   "DC Public Library Celebrates 125 Years of Service," DC Public Library, https://www.dclibrary.org/125.

2   "Mission and History," DC Public Library, https://www.dclibrary.org/about /mission.

3   "Staff," DC Public Library, https://www.dclibrary.org/about/staff.

4   Institute of Museum and Library Services. Library Search & Compare, https:// www.imls.gov/search-compare/details.html?fscs_id=DC0001.

5   Seena Fazel et al., "The Prevalence of Mental Disorders Among the Homeless in Western Countries: Systematic Review and Meta-Regression Analysis," *PLOS Medicine* 5, no. 12: e225, https://doi.org/10.1371/journal .pmed.0050225.

6: Cold Mercy

1 "The History of Homelessness in the United States," appendix B in *Permanent Supportive Housing: Evaluating the Evidence for Improving Health Outcomes Among People Experiencing Chronic Homelessness* (Washington, DC: National Academies Press, 2018), https://www.ncbi.nlm.nih.gov/books/NBK519584/.

2 Bruce Katz, "Racial Division and Concentrated Poverty in U.S. Cities" (PowerPoint presentation, Urban Age Conference, Johannesburg, South Africa, 2006), https://www.brookings.edu/wp-content/uploads/2016/06/20060707_UrbanAge.pdf.

3 "History of Homelessness in the United States."

4 John F. Kennedy, "Special Message on Mental Illness and Mental Retardation," White House Fish Room, February 5, 1963, JFK Library, https://www.jfklibrary.org/asset-viewer/archives/JFKPOF/052/JFKPOF-052-012.

5 Daniel Yohanna, "Deinstitutionalization of People with Mental Illness: Causes and Consequences," *Virtual Mentor* 15, no. 10 (2013): 886–891, https://doi.org/10.1001/virtualmentor.2013.15.10.mhst1-1310.

6 "Reflecting on JFK's Legacy of Community-Based Care," SAMHSA, updated March 18, 2021, https://www.samhsa.gov/homelessness-programs-resources/hpr-resources/jfks-legacy-community-based-care.

7 Darold Treffert, "Dying with Their Rights On," *American Journal of Psychiatry* 130, no. 9: 1041, https://doi.org/10.1176/ajp.130.9.1041.

8 Treatment Advocacy Center, *Overlooked in the Undercounted: The Role of Mental Illness in Fatal Law Enforcement Encounters*, 2015, https://www.treatmentadvocacycenter.org/overlooked-in-the-undercounted.

9 "Mental Health by the Numbers," NAMI, updated March 2021, https://www.nami.org/mhstats.

10 "'Insane': America's 3 Largest Psychiatric Facilities Are Jails," KCUR 89.3—NPR in Kansas City, April 30, 2018, https://www.kcur.org/2018-04-30/insane-americas-3-largest-psychiatric-facilities-are-jails.

11 Justin Wm. Moyer, "Franklin Square to Close for Year-Long Renovation," *Washington Post*, June 26, 2020, www.washingtonpost.com/local/franklin-square-to-close-for-year-long-renovation/2020/06/26/06f6c0b4-b7b7-11ea-9b0f-c797548c1154_story.html.

12   Moyer, "Franklin Square to Close for Year-Long Renovation."

13   HUD, "PIT and HIC Data Since 2007," HUD Exchange. https://www.hudexchange .info/resource/3031/pit-and-hic-data-since-2007/.

14   HUD, "PIT and HIC Data Since 2007."

15   US Census Bureau "QuickFacts: District of Columbia," April 1, 2020, https:// www.census.gov/quickfacts/fact/table/DC/POP010220.

16   Hana Burkly, "Washington DC, USA: An Urban Design and Mental Health Case Study," *Journal of Urban Design and Mental Health* 6, no. 13 (2020), https://www.urbandesignmentalhealth.com/journal-6-washingtondc.html.

17   Marcia Slacum Greene, "Homeless Sheltered at RFK Stadium," *Washington Post*, March 23, 1988, https://www.washingtonpost.com/archive/local/1988/03/23 /homeless-sheltered-at-rfk-stadium/97843cec-5cbe-4220-a708-107c096e9f20/.

18   "A Judge's Order," *Washington Post*, January 20, 1989, https://www .washingtonpost.com/archive/opinions/1989/01/20/a-judges-order/2857038b -50f9-4bde-bf1e-38a7988899dc/?utm_term=.686e3b04d322.

19   Meeting Minutes dated September 19, 1984, of the Coalition for the Home-less, Carol Fennelly Personal Papers, box 28, folder 16, Gelman Library Spe-cial Collections, George Washington University in Washington, DC.

20   Katie J. Wells, "Policy-Failing: A Repealed Right to Shelter," *Urban Geog-raphy* 41, no. 9 (2020): 1139–1157, https://doi.org/10.1080/02723638.2019 .1598733.

21   Martin Austermuhle, "In Wake of MLK Library Closure, D.C. Officials Scramble to Find Alternatives for Homeless," WAMU, March 8, 2017, https:// wamu.org/story/17/03/08/wake-mlk-library-closure-d-c-officials-scramble -find-alternatives-homeless/.

7: For Whom

1   Marissa Lang, "A D.C. Library Was Closed for More than Two Days After Sev-eral Live Snakes Were Found Inside," *Washington Post*, August 7, 2018, https:// www.washingtonpost.com/local/a-dc-library-was-closed-for-more-than-two -days-after-several-live-snakes-were-found-inside/2018/08/07/36edf17e -9a87-11e8-b60b-1c897f17e185_story.html.

2   General Accounting Office, *Activities of Special Police and Guard Forces in the District of Columbia Can Be Improved: Report* (United States, 1978), https://

www.google.com/books/edition/Activities_of_Special_Police_and_Guard_F
/jH1EcQKXXTEC?hl=en&gbpv=0.

3   Joseph Goldstein, "Dallas Police Chief David Brown, a Reformer, Becomes
     Face of Nation's Shock," *New York Times*, July 9, 2016, https://www.nytimes
     .com/2016/07/09/us/dallas-police-chief-david-brown-a-reformer-becomes
     -face-of-nations-shock.html.

4   "Dallas Police Chief: 'We're Asking Cops to Do Too Much,'" *Denver Post*,
     July 12, 2016, https://www.denverpost.com/2016/07/12/dallas-police-chief
     -were-asking-cops-to-do-too-much/.

8: Burning Out

1   Leslie Jamison, *The Empathy Exams: Essays* (Minneapolis: Graywolf Press, 2014).

2   Carla Joinson, "Coping with Compassion Fatigue, *Nursing* 22 (1992): 116–120.

3   "Empathy Fatigue: How Stress and Trauma Can Take a Toll on You," Health
     Essentials from Cleveland Clinic, June 25, 2021, https://health.clevelandclinic
     .org/empathy-fatigue-how-stress-and-trauma-can-take-a-toll-on-you/.

4   Yasmin Anwar, "Researcher Takes on 'Empathy Fatigue' in the Workplace," *Berke-
     ley News*, July 9, 2015, https://news.berkeley.edu/2011/12/06/compassionfatigue/.

PART III: RECKONING

9: An Education

1   US Census Bureau, "QuickFacts: Riverside City, California," July 1, 2019, https://
     www.census.gov/quickfacts/fact/table/riversidecitycalifornia/PST045219.

10: Libraries Will (Not) Save Us

1   Neil Gaiman, "Why Our Future Depends on Libraries, Reading and Day-
     dreaming," *Guardian*, October 15, 2013, https://www.theguardian.com
     /books/2013/oct/15/neil-gaiman-future-libraries-reading-daydreaming.

2   David Kipen, "How to Weather the Trump Administration: Head to the
     Library," *Los Angeles Times*, November 10, 2016, https://www.latimes.com
     /books/jacketcopy/la-ca-jc-kipen-essay-20161110-story.html.

3   Ellen McGirt, "Librarians Will Save Us All," *Fortune*, May 22, 2017, https://
     fortune.com/2017/05/22/librarians-will-save-us-all/.

4   Eric Klinenberg, "How Libraries Can Save the 2020 Election," *New York Times*, September 3, 2020, https://www.nytimes.com/2020/09/03/opinion/mail-voting-trump-libraries.html.

5   Ellen Rosen, "Beyond the Pandemic, Libraries Look Toward a New Era," *New York Times*, September 24, 2020, https://www.nytimes.com/2020/09/24/business/libraries-pandemic-future.html.

6   Deborah Fallows, "Public Libraries Respond to COVID-19," Our Towns, *Atlantic*, March 31, 2020, https://www.theatlantic.com/notes/2020/03/public-libraries-novel-response-to-a-novel-virus/609058/.

7   Deborah Fallows, "When Libraries Are 'Second Responders,'" Our Towns, *Atlantic*, May 23, 2019, https://www.theatlantic.com/notes/2019/05/when-libraries-are-second-responders/590098/.

8   Fallows, "Public Libraries Respond to COVID-19."

9   Donna Braquet, "Library Experiences of Hurricane Katrina and New Orleans Flood Survivors," *Libres* 20, no. 1 (March 2010), https://www.libres-ejournal.info/528/.

10 Bibi Alajmi, "When the Nation Is in Crisis: Libraries Respond," *Library Management* 37, no. 8/9 (November 2016): 465–481, https://doi.org/10.1108/LM-05-2016-0043.

11 Loida Garcia-Febo, "Rebuilding Puerto Rican Libraries," *American Libraries*, February 1, 2018, https://americanlibrariesmagazine.org/2018/02/01/rebuilding-puerto-rican-libraries/.

12 Catherine Lemann, "AIDS and Public Libraries: A Look Back and a Look Forward," *American Libraries* 32, no. 4 (Summer 1993): 505–514.

13 Leonard Kniffel, "Getting to Know Islam," editorial, *American Libraries* 33, no. 1 (2002): 48, http://www.jstor.org/stable/25646184.

14 Alajmi, "When the Nation Is in Crisis."

15 Alajmi, "When the Nation Is in Crisis."

16 Scott G. Allen, Larra Clark, Michele Coleman, Lynn Silipigni Connaway, Chris Cyr, Kendra Morgan, and Mercy Procaccini, *Libraries Respond to the Opioid Crisis with Their Communities: Summary Report* (Dublin, OH: OCLC, 2019), https://doi.org/10.25333/qgrn-hj36.

17 Lauren Holmes, "Anchorage Moves Its Emergency Operations Center into Loussac Library," *Anchorage Daily News*, March 27, 2020, https://

www.adn.com/alaska-news/anchorage/2020/03/27/anchorage-moves-its -emergency-operations-center-into-the-loussac-library/.

18 Lisa Peet, "Budgeting for the New Normal: Libraries Respond to COVID-19 Funding Constraints," *Library Journal*, September 24, 2020, https://www .libraryjournal.com?detailStory=budgeting-for-the-new-normal-libraries -respond-to-covid-19-funding-constraints.

19 "How Search Organizes Information," Google, https://www.google.com /search/howsearchworks/crawling-indexing/.

20 Jonathan Zittrain, "The Internet Is Rotting," *Atlantic*, June 30, 2021, https://www.theatlantic.com/technology/archive/2021/06/the-internet-is-a -collective-hallucination/619320/.

21 Zittrain, "The Internet Is Rotting."

22 "No Longer a Refuge for Readers : Libraries Are Trying Off-Duty Police, Security Cameras to Counter Rising Crime. The Numbers of Street People Seeking Shelter Have Prompted Use of Such Extreme Measures as Odor Monitors," *Los Angeles Times*, August 10, 1993, https://www.latimes.com /archives/la-xpm-1993-08-10-mn-22346-story.html.

23 Carl Ingram, "Killer Spoke of His Wife Before Being Slain, Police Say," *Los Angeles Times*, April 20, 1993, https://www.latimes.com/archives/la-xpm -1993-04-20-mn-25067-story.html.

24 Storm Gifford, "Murder Suspect Arrested in Shooting Death of California Librarian," *NY Daily News*, December 14, 2018, https://www.nydailynews .com/news/national/ny-news-ronald-seay-charged-with-killing-librarian -20181214-story.html.

25 "Sentencing Hearing Begins for Teen in Clovis Library Shooting," KRQE NEWS 13, New Mexico, February 11, 2019, https://www.krqe.com/news /new-mexico/sentencing-hearing-begins-for-teen-in-clovis-library-shooting/.

26 Travis Andersen, "Winchester Library Stabbing Suspect Was Diagnosed with Schizophrenia, Lawyer Says," *Boston Globe*, April 11, 2018, https://www .bostonglobe.com/metro/2018/04/11/alleged-killer-woman-inside-winchester -library-diagnosed-with-schizophrenia-lawyer-says/kbXkoWX5LSZtca25Fm7U3H /story.html.

27 "Fort Myers Beach Library Director Stabbed to Death," NBC2 News, January 23, 2019, https://nbc-2.com/nbc-2-wbbh/2019/01/23/fort-myers-beach -library-director-stabbed-to-death/.

28 Kelly Clark, "Keep Library Workers Safe," *American Libraries*, April 23, 2019, https://americanlibrariesmagazine.org/2019/04/23/keep-library -workers-safe/.

29 Katie McLain, "Essential Until We're Not: The Disregard for Library Staff Safety," *Book Riot*, May 20, 2020, https://bookriot.com/library-staff-safety/.

11: Multiphrenia

1 Pew Research Center: Internet, Science & Tech, *Demographics of Social Media Users and Adoption in the United States* (survey of US adults conducted January 25–February 8, 2021), https://www.pewresearch.org/internet/fact-sheet /social-media/.

2 Anamika Barman-Adhikari and Jaih Craddock, "How We Can Leverage Social Networks, Tech to Help Homeless Young," *Youth Today*, September 24, 2019, https://youthtoday.org/2019/09/how-we-can-leverage-social -networks-tech-to-help-homeless-young/.

3 William Deresiewicz, "Solitude and Leadership" (lecture, United States Military Academy at West Point, in October 2009), https://www.montana.edu /parents/resources--old/Solitude%20and%20Leadership.pdf.

4 John Kenneth Galbraith, *The Affluent Society*, (Boston: Houghton Mifflin, 1998).

5 Kenneth Burke, *The Philosophy of Literary Form. Studies in Symbolic Action* (New York: Vintage Books, 1961).

6 Katherine Miller, "The 2010s Have Broken Our Sense of Time," *BuzzFeed News*, October 24, 2019, https://www.buzzfeednews.com/article/katherinemiller /the-2010s-have-broken-our-sense-of-time.

7 Kenneth J. Gergen, *The Saturated Self: Dilemmas of Identity in Contemporary Life* (New York: Basic Books, 1991).

8 Dan Baum, "The Following Account of My Short Career at the New Yorker Ran as a Series of Tweets on May 8, 11, and 12, 2009," https://danbaum .files.wordpress.com/2018/03/new-yorker-tweets.pdf.

9 David Kushner, "Zola Tells All: The Story Behind the Greatest Stripper Saga Ever Tweeted," *Rolling Stone*, November 17, 2015, https://www.rollingstone .com/feature/zola-tells-all-the-real-story-behind-the-greatest-stripper-saga -ever-tweeted-73048/.

10 Lyz Lenz, "Thread Man," *Columbia Journalism Review*, February 11, 2021, https://www.cjr.org/special_report/seth-abramson-twitter.php/.

11   Aja Romano, "Why We Can't Stop Fighting About Cancel Culture," *Vox*, December 30, 2019, https://www.vox.com/culture/2019/12/30/20879720 /what-is-cancel-culture-explained-history-debate.

12   Ligaya Mishan, "The Long and Tortured History of Cancel Culture," *New York Times*, December 3, 2020, https://www.nytimes.com/2020/12/03/t -magazine/cancel-culture-history.html.

13   Romano, "Why We Can't Stop Fighting About Cancel Culture."

14   Charles Taylor, *A Secular Age* (London: Belknap Press, 2018).

15   Jonah Engel Bromwich, "Everyone Is Canceled," *New York Times*, June 28, 2018, https://www.nytimes.com/2018/06/28/style/is-it-canceled.html.

16   Mishan, "Long and Tortured History of Cancel Culture."

17   Robin Wall Kimmerer, *Braiding Sweetgrass* (Minneapolis: Milkweed Editions, 2015).

12: The Future of the American Public Library

1   Rebecca Solnit, *Hope in the Dark: Untold Histories, Wild Possibilities* (Chicago: Haymarket Books, 2016), 138–139.

2   "Age-Adjusted Mortality Rate for Sheltered Homeless New Yorkers," Coalition for the Homeless, accessed July 18, 2021, https://www.coalitionforthehomeless .org/age-adjusted-mortality-rate-for-sheltered-homeless-new-yorkers/.

3   James Baldwin, "As Much Truth as One Can Bear," *New York Times*, January 14, 1962.

4   Adrienne Maree Brown, "Vegas and Everything Else," blog post, October 2, 2017, http://adriennemareebrown.net/2017/10/02/vegas-and-everything-else/.

5   Clarice Lispector, Água Viva (New York: New Directions, 2012.)

INDEX